BLESSINGS
of Forgiveness

THE LIFE
OF EVANJELICA,
A SURVIVOR

Blessings of Forgiveness: The Life of Evanjelica, A Survivor
Copyright ©2020 Maria Rio

All rights reserved. No part of this book may be used or reproduced in any manner whatsoever, including Internet usage, without written permission from the publisher and/or author, except in the case of brief quotations embodied in critical articles and reviews.

Interior Layout and Cover Design by Melissa Williams Design
Cover art: David Parrish of David Parrish Design

BLESSINGS
of Forgiveness

THE LIFE
OF EVANJELICA,
A SURVIVOR

BY MARIA RIO

To My Family

Table of Contents

Survivor ii
Introduction v
Chapter One 1
Chapter Two 7
Chapter Three 12
Chapter Four 15
Chapter Five 21
Chapter Six 24
Chapter Seven 29
Chapter Eight 33
Chapter Nine 39
Chapter Ten 48
Chapter Eleven 54
Chapter Twelve 57
Chapter Thirteen 62
Chapter Fourteen 71
Chapter Fifteen 79
Chapter Sixteen 85
Chapter Seventeen 98
Chapter Eighteen 102
Chapter Nineteen 108
Chapter Twenty 117
Chapter Twenty-one 128
Chapter Twenty-two 141
Chapter Twenty-three 147
Acknowledgements 152
About the Author 153

Survivor

The life of Evanjelica,
she is daughter of GOD.
Her scars tell a story when life
tried to break her, but FAILED.

This novel is the perfect example
in the journey towards
your greatest ambitions.
We all encounter challenges in life,
some more so than others.

Evanjelica is a true warrior, a leader,
and a perfect role model for women,
mothers, and single working parents.
She did it all, and alone, with no regrets.

Life threw many stones at her,
she tripped on many bumpy roads,
she fell many times, but always managed
to get herself up. Her life took many wrong turns.
She never gave up, held her head high up,
her heart wide open.

Her bad childhood, her bad marriage,
her bad breakup, her life after divorce,
her world crumbled down, like evil warfare.
She got discouraged from time to time,
but never was defeated.

She had a sense of purpose in life
to raise her children, as she always said,
children did not ask to come into this world.
She put them here, it is her responsibility to raise
them with or without help until they grow

wings to fly solo to pursue their dreams.
Her determination helped her overcome obstacles.

Patient protection against wrongs.
Perseverance is a great element of success.
Purpose gives confidence to face each new
day with courage.

Introduction

Note to Readers:
Every single word in this book is true

Who is Evanjelica? What Kind of Woman is She? This is Her Story

Evanjelica may have suffered her entire life, but she will never be defeated. She is humble, kind, and tireless, going above and beyond to help anyone in need—she does everything from the kindness of her heart.

In this book, she shares her life story about how she survived injustice and overcame obstacles: a missing mother, an abusive father and stepmother, and an abusive husband, who when they divorced, continued his abuse toward Evanjelica. His new wife also played a large role in this abusive behavior. Perhaps you are going through a similar situation of domestic abuse or a dysfunctional family—please know that you are not alone. You CAN change your circumstances and you will find the strength to succeed with the help of supportive family and friends. Evanjelica is proof of that. Her children kept her going. She worked hard to feed them and she stayed strong for them. Ultimately, Evanjelica believes in the power of forgiveness, which is so strong, it will help us be at peace with our conscience and will eventually even change our enemy's stubborn hearts.

She prays daily for the safety and protection of her children and grandchildren, and she prays for her enemies to be blessed with everything good. Maybe one day they will come to their senses and realize how much damage and pain they have caused; they will amend their lives and become better people. Evanjelica's wish is for everybody to be happy and surrounded with love, prosperity, abundance, happiness, and respect. It breaks her heart to see so much pain and see so many innocent children, animals, and people in general suffering and enduring abuse. Yet, God works in mysterious ways; whatever the seed we plant most likely will be the fruit we will reap. If you feed a hungry person in need, tomorrow you might be that same hungry person in need and someone else will feed you. It may not be same person you previously fed, but your good deeds will come back to you.

HARD LESSONS LEARNED

Because Evanjelica is biracial she has been discriminated against, harassed her entire life, and when she became a mother she knew she had to confront anybody or anything to protect her children. It was her motherly instincts that gave her the courage to finally speak up, which was a big shock for her bullies who started to call her crazy. She was not crazy when they needed her help to better themselves; she was not crazy when she swallowed all the abuse and insults; but, she was crazy when she started hitting them back with the truth. Some people enjoy going around destroying other people's lives with lies. They don't realize that, sooner or later, their own life can be destroyed with truth and so they're not prepared for it.

Over the course of many trials, Evanjelica learned to never be afraid of losing fake friends because having one fake friend is worse having than ten enemies. Or sometimes being alone is better than being miserable. Along with this, negative surroundings are never healthy; gain the strength and courage to break free and move away when others are trying to drag you down. Be a leader not a follower. If you want to be a follower, choose wisely. If you follow a good person, make sure they are honest and someone who commits good deeds so you can become better than them and remain a good soul. On the other hand, if you follow the wrong crowds, you will become worse than a single bad rotten apple.

A good person will succeed alone without any help because they are focused on the good things that will help them succeed. A bad person can't succeed alone because they need help from a partner and friends. Bullies only have power when they feel supported by their followers; once they are alone nobody will help them, and they won't know what to do with themselves. Some people like to be the center of attention all over social media by slandering other people who have helped them get a better life. That is why they intimidate you to bring you down to their level. Do not lower your standards to please false prophets; be yourself and walk tall. Bullies are not more important than you or anybody else; they are just miserable and unhappy.

Evanjelica is a leader who has many friends, but she chooses her friends wisely—those who are loyal, honest, and willing to tell the truth to her face. She knows the truth hurts and nobody likes to hear it, but she is a strong woman and can handle the truth; this is the kind of friend she is and these are the kinds of friends she chooses in her life. For over thirty years her friends have seen Evanjelica's ups and downs, smiles and tears, and they have never abandoned her. They stand by her side when she is struggling and are there to celebrate her successes.

She separated herself from friends who smiled at her but stabbed her in the back. Unfortunately, there are lot of those "friends" out there, and they can be the cause of a family's destruction. A happy, successful person does not harass or intimidate others; a happy person will help you in your time of need and is happy to see you succeed. Evanjelica learned that you can't change the past, but you can change the future and change the way you think so you can learn from your mistakes.

When the world turns its back at you, don't turn your back on the world. Evanjelica felt like the world closed all its doors to her, but she didn't feel discouraged; she didn't need the world in her life. All she needs is the One, the One who is in control of the world.

Evanjelica always wanted to speak her side of the story, yet she didn't because she wanted to avoid confrontation; however, she then realized that the wrong thing to say was to say nothing at all. We should all have the freedom to speak up and stand up for our rights. This book was born from Evanjelica's longing to tell her story. She realized that her life matters, your life matters, as we are all God's creation, and we are all valuable human beings. We can all learn from each other's humanity.

Thank you for reading this book and Evanjelica hopes it brings hope and blessings into your life.

Chapter One

Evanjelica's father, Ernesto Alexander, was full Portuguese, her paternal grandparents were both Portuguese, and her mother, Maria da Luz Lencastro, was half Black African and white German; *da Luz* is Portuguese and means "light" in English. Evanjelica's maternal grandfather was German and he was killed when Maria da Luz was an infant. Evanjelica's maternal grandmother was African, born in Angola during the time of slavery when Black people and mixed people were discriminated against, forced to do hard work, and starved and beaten.

Ernesto left his country, Portugal, right after his military service and traveled for a month on a boat to Africa. He found himself employment with the *minerio*/mine in Dondo, Angola, where he worked a few years.

Maria da Luz also lived in Dondo and she was a single mom of two young children: a boy, Mauricio Lencastro, and girl, Carmo Lencastro. Their father had died. Maria da Luz's mother, Victoria Sofia, helped her with her kids.

One day in 1959, Luz and Ernesto crossed paths. This young white handsome man was immediately attracted to Maria da Luz, who was also young and an incredibly stunning half-black woman. They start dating and decided to build a life together. In mid-May of 1960, while still living in Dondo, their first-born son, Agostinho Lencastro Alexander, was born.

Two years later, Ernesto had saved enough money from his hard work at the *minerio* to invest in properties. He purchased this big piece of land filled with coffee bean bushes in the suburbs near the city of N'dalatando, also known as Salazar. He had some of the bushes cut down to build a house on the other half of the property.

LIFE WITH MOM AND DAD, 1962 TO 1964

When Maria da Luz was pregnant with her second child, the apartment in Dondo was very small, so they rented a bigger house in Luanda, the capital of Angola, for two years while their house in N'dalatando was being built. Luanda used to be known as Sao Paulo when it was founded in 1576 by the Portuguese explorer, Paulo Dias de Novais.

In early spring of March of 1962, in Luanda, their second child, a baby girl, was born. Evanjelica Lencastro Alexander was born premature and was so exceedingly small Ernesto and Maria da Luz rushed to baptize the baby girl because they didn't know if she would survive. They needed godparents. Maria da Luz's godmother had a married son, who was a doctor, and an unmarried daughter. They were already godparents to their older child, Agostinho. So they used the same single godmother and one of Ernesto's single male friends, Tomas Rodrigues.

Ernesto thought maybe they could play matchmaker and get the two single people to date, but instead Tomas was attracted to Maria da Luz. Tomas knew Maria da Luz was in a relationship, and he respected her. He also knew Ernesto was a jealous, possessive, and violent man. Tomas Rodrigues was a decent man and would never be the reason to cause tension between a couple or break up a family. Shortly after baptizing the baby girl, Tomas moved away to Portugal, and he later became aware of Ernesto's infidelity to Maria da Luz and could not bear to see Ernesto abusing her, the woman he still had feelings for. It took him a while to get over Luz. He knew a relationship with Luz would be impossible since she had a family and was loyal to Ernesto.

Tomas ended his contact with Ernesto completely and then got married. He did not see his goddaughter Evanjelica grow up; the last time he saw her she was toddler. He never expected to ever see the family again until one day many years later he saw Evanjelica in Portugal as a woman when she went to get married. He thought she was Maria da Luz because she looked so much like her mother.

They caught up on each other's lives and she invited Tomas to her wedding, and then asked him why she never saw him growing up. He then explained what had happened. "Thank you for inviting me, but I don't want ruin your special day. It would be a conflict if I see your father. I disapprove of his behavior with your mother." Tomas did not want to face Ernesto, who'd left her mother back in Angola for another woman, Demonesa, Evanjelica's stepmother.

Ernesto kept moving around every couple of years as he started to invest in more properties. Their house in N'dalatando was finally finished. It was a beautiful brick home with enough land around for vegetables and a flower garden. The couple and young children moved in and Maria da Luz soon became pregnant with Ernesto's third child.

Early in March of 1964 in N'dalatando, a baby boy, Gabriel Lencastro Alexander, was born. Time passed and the children started to grow. Ernesto spent a lot of time traveling for work while Maria da Luz stayed home and took care of the kids and house. She made clothing for her children and also sewed garments for extra income. While Ernesto traveled, he got himself busy meeting many women, dropping his pants, planting his seeds around Angola, and causing much tension when he came back home.

Evanjelica reached the age of five in time to start kindergarten in August 1967. Due to her prematurity, she was exceedingly small for her age and got bullied a lot in school, but she was "brain" smart. Things at home got uncomfortable every time her father came home. He became more abusive to her mom and to her siblings as well. Maria da Luz was an attractive woman, loyal to her husband and devoted to her family, while Ernesto was very insecure and very jealous of her. Ernesto was not only meeting women on his travels, but he had also already fathered some children with different women. His jealousy of Maria da Luz turned physical and verbally abusive because he didn't trust her and believed no man could look at her without it meaning she was cheating on him. He used to hit and kick her in front of the children leaving her bleeding; he broke her ribs. The kids were very scared and traumatized.

THE OTHER WOMAN

Luz asked her mother if she could send her older daughter Carmo from her previous marriage to live with her. Because of her injuries, she needed Carmo's help to care for the youngest children. When the school year ended, Luz took all the kids, Carmo, age 13, and the three smaller children, Agostinho, eight, Evanjelica, six, and Gabriel, four, to Camoma, just 15 kilometers away in order to confront Demonesa, whom she suspected of sleeping with her husband. Demonesa also had three small children, one boy, Alessandro, and two girls, Maya and Zelda.

MARIA DA LUZ STARTED BEATING DEMONESA, THEN RETURNED HOME.

That day Ernesto came home at 5 p.m., a little earlier than usual and started beating Luz with a baseball bat—the kids didn't know why he was doing this. She was bleeding all over. He tied her hands and feet with rope and told the children he was going to throw her in the Rio Kwanza with the alligators. That day the closest neighbors, a married couple, were not at home, so they did not hear or see the incident. The children were crying, scared, and traumatized.

Then Carmo gathered all the small children into the same room. She told them, "We are going to wait for him to come back, and if he does not bring Mom back, we will jump out of the window and run to the police." Around midnight, he came back home. They looked out the window to see him pulling their mom out of the trunk of his truck and dragging her from the driveway to the back of the house. He walked into house, kicked the bedroom door open, and forbade the children from feeding her or giving her any water to drink. He said, "She must die out there slowly." The kids did not know why he treated their mom that way. What did she do that was that bad? Of course later they found out the reason. Ernesto had passed by the other woman's house first and she complained about Luz beating her. Demonesa later became Evanjelica's stepmother.

MOM AND DAD'S SEPARATION, 1968 TO 1969

That night the kids did not sleep. Evanjelica was very traumatized and kept telling Carmo, her older sister, "What if a snake or wild animal eats Mom?" The next morning Ernesto went to work in town and did not travel for work all week.

Because Angola is located in the tropics, Carmo fed Luz and gave her water to drink so she would not get dehydrated. Luz still had her hands and feet tied up. When Ernesto came home he grabbed a piece of wood with nails to beat Carmo. She was screaming and bleeding while the younger children were all frantic and screaming. Thankfully, the neighbors happened to be home and heard the screaming. Both the husband and wife came over. The husband, a very tall and big man, grabbed Ernesto, pinned him down and they waited for the police. The wife untied Luz and started to treat Luz and Carmo's wounds.

With Ernesto gone, Luz gathered some of her things, such as her sewing machine, and she, Carmo, and all the children got on a bus and left the house that she'd helped their father build. She did not know she was a few weeks' pregnant with their fourth child.

Ernesto was only in jail a week. Since he was rich and powerful he always got himself out.

On the bus, the passengers saw Luz and Carmo all bandaged up and bleeding. They questioned them and offered to help. Maria da Luz decided to go back and live in Dondo where she had some friends. Evanjelica's mother and sister, who had just turned 14, both got jobs at the local factory close to home.

LIFE WITH MOM IN DONDO, 1968

At age six, Evanjelica saw her mom struggle financially but she was happy. The neighbors were good and kind, and the house was peaceful.

As time passed. Maria da Luz's belly started to show. And when they thought all was peaceful and safe, Ernesto found out where they lived; since he traveled a lot, it was easy for him to find them.

He saw that Maria da Luz was pregnant and he immediately thought she'd cheated on him. He started beating her. The neighbors came to help and chased Ernesto out. Ernesto wanted to take all the children with him, but he could not as they were in school. Evanjelica had started first grade and Agostinho, her older brother, was repeating second grade. Their father would stop by for the occasional visit and take the kids out to eat.

A few months went by, and at the end of school year Ernesto took the kids away from their mother.

She had already given birth to a new baby boy, Armando, and even though he looked like his father and the two older boys, Ernesto refused to accept him as his child. He took the kids from their mother. Everyone was crying and heart-broken to leave her behind, and she could not fight back because he was violent and strong. The kids were afraid of him. Evanjelica had just turned seven, Agostinho was nine, and Gabriel, the younger brother, was five years old.

They spent a week in a car with their father traveling before they reached their destination. When they finally arrived at his new house, Evanjelica immediately recognized the Black woman her mom had fought with. She had a good memory with faces.

Ernesto's older brother, Jeronimo Alexander, also lived in Angola with his wife and four children, three girls and one boy. Jeronimo did not approve of Ernesto's behavior of abusing Maria da Luz and cheating on her with prostitutes. The two brothers often bumped heads and they were the only two from their family living in Africa away from Portugal. They would sometimes go months, even years, without talking to each other. Ernesto was a hardworking and successful man; too bad he had such a horrible temper.

Chapter Two

Life with the Stepmother, 1968 to 1975

Ernesto took his children from their mother to go live with him and his mistress Demonesa Lucifrano and her three children: her son, Alessandro, and her two girls, Maya and Zelda. She later became his wife. Ernesto continued to travel a great deal for work and would spend one full week out on the road. Life with a stepmother was hell.

Demonesa Lucifrano was a Black African female sorcerer who practiced witchcraft and dark black magic. When she first met Ernesto, she was pregnant with another man's baby and that man had abandoned her. Ernesto at first didn't know who this woman truly was until later when he intended to leave her after he caught her cheating. Demonesa then told Ernesto, "You knew I was a prostitute and I know you just wanted to have fun for one night. But you were different than all the other men and I wanted to keep you and I did. I became pregnant by another man and when I told him he told me he would never be with someone like me. So, I paralyzed him, and he has not been able to walk or move his arms for a few years. I know what I did, and he'll never move again."

Ernesto told Evanjelica he was planning to leave Demonesa behind with her son because he was too embarrassed to present her to his family in Portugal and because she cheated on him. Demonesa somehow either overheard this conversation or just guessed his plans. She confronted Ernesto telling him, "I'll do the same thing to you as I did to my son's father." Ernesto chickened out and ended up bringing her and her son to Portugal. Ernesto kept telling Evanjelica that he loved her mother and couldn't stop thinking of her, but he didn't know what was happening to him since Demonesa had power over him. Evanjelica was a little girl and too young to understand any of this adult stuff until later in life when her grandaunt told her how her father had abused her mother.

Before Evanjelica even had a chance to say anything about what her father told her, her grandaunt told Evanjelica, "My nephew is under a voodoo spell and it is impossible for him, who is my blood, to behave the way he did with your mother, which is so violent."

She continued. "I know for a fact that some white Portuguese men from this town of Santa Cruz were married here and went to Africa alone to make money to better themselves. They ended up getting involved with Black African women. When they came back to visit their wives, who loved and respected them, these men were extremely violent and abusive to their wives and children here in Santa Cruz." She told Evanjelica there was no other explanation for her father to treat her mother that way unless he was under a strong spell. As a young teenage girl Evanjelica was even more confused. She hoped her grandaunt was right and maybe with time life could explain some things to her, such as the reasons behind people's actions, because, after all, life is our best teacher.

Evanjelica was practically a slave to her stepmother Demonesa and her kids. Many times, when she came home from school she found her two stepsisters, Maya, age three, and Zelda, a year old, were left home alone. Evanjelica had to change diapers, do the laundry, clean, cook, and feed all of her siblings. Demonesa was always out and about; she never worked, and there wasn't any reason for her not to be home with her children. Ernesto suspected that she was cheating on him. The neighbors would tell him that the children were home alone a lot. He would ask Evanjelica if she ever saw Demonesa with any men. She answered, "No, I never have. She is just never home." Ernesto decided to spy on Demonesa, pretending he was going on a weeklong trip for work, his usual routine, but stayed a few blocks away from the house.

On the first night he hid behind the bushes and on the second night, when he was supposedly on his trip, he saw a guy walk into the house. He waited a couple of hours and the guy never came out. At midnight, Ernesto walked in and caught this man in bed with Demonesa. This man was her cousin and Demonesa was pregnant with his baby. Evanjelica's father started beating both of them and as a result of this beating, she did lose the baby.

Meanwhile, the children were sleeping not knowing what was going on, but they soon woke up from all the noise and screaming. Demonesa and the cousin ended up in the hospital while Ernesto went to jail. By the next day he was released.

Evanjelica asked her father why he was home so early. Wasn't he was supposed be on a trip for a week? Ernesto then told her the story, that he never left town because he wanted to spy on her stepmother from behind the bushes. While her stepmother was recuperating all those months, Ernesto placed nine-year-old Evanjelica in charge of the house to do all the cooking, cleaning, and caring for the youngest children. That was supposed to be her school vacation; while all the other kids were out playing she was taking care of her family and siblings. She cried a lot wishing her mom was with her.

PUNISHMENT FOR HER FATHER

Ernesto abused Maria da Luz, an honest, decent woman, and he cheated on her with Demonesa, who only cared for his money, and who in turn cheated on him with her own cousin.

After three months, when Demonesa returned from the hospital, she became very abusive to Evanjelica and her two brothers. She began to beat them for no reason—maybe to get revenge on their father and mom. When Ernesto got home Demonesa just blamed Evanjelica for random things so her father could hit her and her brothers again.

Maria da Luz kept visiting her children when she could, yet

because she did not drive it was hard for her as she had to depend on others for rides. It was sad to see her mom leave, but it was also sad she could not take the kids with her.

With all the drama happening at her house, Evanjelica was also being bullied at school with no one to protect her. She was small for her age, but was very smart in class and never failed any exams, which was the cause of all the bullying.

Evanjelica's first year of middle school was extremely hard. She was only 10 years old and spent the summer caring for her younger siblings. With all the problems at home and bullying at school, she was extremely exhausted and got very skinny and sick. Her father took her to the hospital. Evanjelica was admitted for three weeks with malaria, which is caused by the Plasmodium parasite through a bite from infected mosquitoes; it causes muscle paralysis. She developed a high fever and it kept getting worse. This was back in the day when there was no knowledge about what proper medication could cure malaria. The doctor told Ernesto, "Your daughter is dying and there's nothing else we can do for her. You can take her home." Ernesto carried Evanjelica in his arms as she was too weak to walk, almost paralyzed from disease. Ernesto could not bear losing his daughter and had to find a way to save her.

Ernesto heard of this woman who was a healer who used home remedies. He took Evanjelica to see this woman who prepared this awful-tasting tea from the roots of plants and herbs. Evanjelica drank it as the woman also rendered a paste of ashes, vinegar, and plants, and covered Evanjelica's body with it.

After a few days, Evanjelica's fever went down, and she slowly started regaining her appetite and strength until she was completely healed. Ernesto was not yet convinced and took his daughter back to the doctor who was surprised to see her walking without a fever—she was cured. However, her stepmother did not care if she was sick, the house chores were waiting for her.

During recess at school, Evanjelica would sit alone on the corner reading and studying; she never played with the other students because of the bullying and she was also sad from all the problems at home. After school she walked home and feared that the bullies would follow and hurt her.

One day she had a big test coming up, so she, as usual, sat in the corner studying while all the other kids were playing. Then she noticed four bullies, two boys and two girls approaching her. She became nervous thinking that they were going to hurt her. To her surprise, they asked her for help instead. They had failing grades while she was a straight A student. Evanjelica said, "Sit and study with me." She helped them solve questions and helped them with math. They aced that test. From that day on they never bullied her again and instead became friends.

Chapter Three

Angola Crisis, Civil War Independence, 1975

On April 25, 1974, a new ruler in Lisbon, Portugal, sought to divest the country of its costly colonial empire, which would make Angola independent. Right after Portugal let go of its control of Angola, the Angolan Crisis began in 1974 and civil war grew into the Cold War, with Cuba's Fidel de Castro intervening. Angolan soldiers had been fighting for this independence since the early 1960s.

In the spring of 1974, Maria da Luz once again came to try to get her kids from Evanjelica's father. This time she did not come alone; she had a few soldiers to protect her from Ernesto. They all went to court. The judge decided to separate the children. Evanjelica and her older brother, Agostinho, went to live with their father, while the younger boy, Gabriel, went to live with his mother, and since Ernesto denied paternity, the baby Armando stayed with his mother. Ernesto was ordered to pay child support which he never did. The war began shortly after they all were separated from each other.

Evanjelica suffered another broken heart, being separated from her mom at age seven and now she was separated from her siblings at age 12. The Crisis continued and it kept getting worse. Things were very tense and scary with much crime, death, starvation, robbery, women and small children being raped and killed, riots everywhere, and the burning down of cars and houses. There was no law and no order.

One night, in the early months of June 1975, at around 8 p.m. the shooting started, and around midnight heavy bombing began in N'dalatando. The Portuguese military started driving around rescuing people to go to the military base. Evanjelica and her family spent 10 days on the military base. There was a lot of shooting and bombing; they slept on the grass, outside of the barracks, with rocks as their pillows, and they were hungry. Most importantly, they had to be alert in order to stay alive.

They were surrounded with Portuguese soldiers who tried to protect all the civilians on base. But they could not fight the Angolan soldiers because the Portuguese president ordered the military to surrender. So, the Portuguese lost their power over Angola.

After 10 days, the Portuguese military helped people get away from the base in N'dalatando to go to Nova Lisboa or New Lisbon. As they were driving out, all cars were being stopped for inspection by soldiers asking if they had money or drugs and where they were heading. During an inspection, one soldier pointed his rifle at Evanjelica and her siblings in the back seat. Evanjelica prayed for this soldier to just pull the trigger and kill her right there inside her father's car. It would be a lot less painful death than to be taken out of the car and raped, tortured, and killed. After a good five minutes of staring at the soldier, he finally changed his mind and walked away from their car. Ernesto drove his family to Nova Lisboa where they stayed for 20 days under the care of the Red Cross.

Evanjelica was not sure if she would ever see her mom or brothers again. They were all refugees of a war and they were still living in Dondo.

In Nova Lisboa, the International Red Cross started the process of taking people out of the country for safety. Ernesto was Portuguese, so their destination would be Portugal. It was a new adventure for all of them except their father, with the children soon living in a country they had never been to.

Evanjelica cried and prayed every day for her mom and siblings who stayed behind. She was just a little girl who had no power to do anything. All she could do was pray for their protection. Leaving Angola was a painful departure from her birth country—painful because she was leaving behind her mother and siblings, and they might never see each other again.

Chapter Four

Life in Portugal, June 1975 to December 1979

Ernesto's parents' house was too small to fit a family of seven. They were separated and went to different family members' homes; his mother was from a big family of many siblings.

Evanjelica was placed in the small town of Santa Cruz Freguesia de Chaves to live with her grandaunt Adelina, her paternal grandma's older sister. She was a widow who had three educated children comprised of one son, and two daughters—all teachers. Her grandchildren were all MDs, surgeons, and lawyers, all living in different cities away from Chaves. Adelina was the second oldest of 19 children from her parents, Evanjelica's paternal great-grandparents, and was the only one of her siblings to have educated her children. Evanjelica learned so much from her, and while living with her grandaunt she was able to finish high school; she had completed her freshman year in Angola, yet had three more years to finish.

Her father did not believe girls should have too much education, and thought Evanjelica was already too smart, that she needed to get married and have babies and not go to school. Ernesto's sister, who was the only girl out of three brothers, had never learned to read or write. Because she had a learning disability, her family had given up on her and thought she was just stupid. Ernesto tried to compare his sister, who was not educated and had married a rich man, to his daughter. Evanjelica told her father, "I don't know if I will marry rich man, but education is important."

Ernesto did not stay in Portugal too long; his younger brother Bernardino lived in the United States for many years as a US citizen, so he made a petition for his two brothers who were refugees from Africa, Ernesto and older brother Jeronimo, along with their wives and kids who also lived in Africa. Ernesto came to America alone for a year, then returned to Portugal to marry Demonesa so he could bring her and her kids to the US. Ernesto's two older children, his son Agostinho and daughter Evanjelica, stayed in Portugal a little while longer. There were immigration issues, so Evanjelica and her brother did not have their mother with them and there were more complications to come.

It benefited Evanjelica to stay with her grandaunt at least until she finished high school, even if she couldn't have any more education. Living with her grandaunt who loved her was good for her and taught her so much; it even made Evanjelica lose interest in going to the US. She was not looking forward to living with her abusive father and stepmother again. Her older brother Agostinho came to the US two years after his stepmother did with her kids, which was six months before Evanjelica did.

Even though she had already graduated high school, Evanjelica wanted to spend Christmas with her grandaunt Adelina, who told her many stories about her family. Adelina's older brother Matews immigrated to the US via boat many years ago in the mid-1940s and because he had papers that were illegal, he traveled by hiding in the coal room and suffered from hunger for a few days. Once Matews reached the US, he worked under the table and got paid cash. When he had enough money saved, he applied for his legal green card. Once established, he was able to slowly bring his family, siblings, nephews, and nieces to the US as legal aliens. He got married, had children, and became a successful homeowner with a few apartment buildings in Massachusetts.

Evanjelica had a great time for the four years she lived with her grandaunt. Her classmate and best friend was Iracema. The girl's parents and siblings, her brother and two sisters, immigrated to France for a better life, while Iracema stayed in Portugal with her grandmother so she could continue to go to school and keep her grandma company. The young girls Evanjelica and Iracema became best friends since they were neighbors, went to school together, saw each other after school, and in the summer. On a school break they would watch the farm animals and vineyard; Iracema and Evanjelica would embroider or crochet while watching over the vineyard to prevent vandalism. Since the vineyards owned by Iracema's grandma and Evanjelica's grandaunt were close to each other, the two girls kept a close eye on the cow, horse, and donkey in the field. The last summer they spent together, Iracema was leaving for college to become a teacher, and Evanjelica was leaving for the United States.

The two women knew eventually they were going to be alone so they started to sell the animals since it would be too much work for an older person to keep up. Even though they had good neighbors willing to help, it was still best to sell the livestock.

Back home, Evanjelica would feed the animals—the chickens, donkey, horse, cow, bunnies, pigs, cat, and dog. Evanjelica liked all the animals her aunt had except the pigs. They always sniffed at her legs getting her all dirty, and that was the life in a small town of Portugal with lots of animals to take care of. After all the animals were fed, she took a shower, and then helped her grandaunt with dinner. After dinner they prayed the Holy Rosary daily, then watched Brazilian telenovelas. Sometimes they just sat near the fireplace, in those special winter months, while her aunt told life stories; some were just funny jokes, and some were real life events concerning her family.

It was just the two of them and they laughed a lot. Time passed; Evanjelica's father sent the documents for her to go to the US embassy in Lisbon to get ready to come to the US. Evanjelica's heart dropped; her grandaunt had just lost her middle daughter to pancreatic cancer. She was a teacher and mother of four children; her older daughter was a teacher and married to a lawyer, while her second oldest son was a single lawyer and her two younger sons were still in school getting their master's degrees. Evanjelica did not want to leave her grandaunt alone. She was happy living with her and really did not want to live with her stepmother again. Yet her father insisted she needed to come as he'd spent too much money on documents and was not going to waste it.

Her grandaunt also encouraged Evanjelica that it was best for her to go to the US because she was an elderly woman in her early eighties and was not going to live much longer, while Evanjelica belonged in the US with her father and siblings. So, Evanjelica took her advice and made sure she had all of her documents ready, yet she wanted to spend Christmas with her grandaunt, and include in the celebration her grandaunt's older daughter, younger son, and all of her grandchildren. Some were married and some were still single, but all of them came to spend Christmas at her grandaunt's and wish Evanjelica a safe trip and good luck in her new life in the US. Her best friend Iracema also came back from college to spend Christmas with her grandma.

It was a happy and sad time because of the goodbyes. Separations from the people we care about is never easy. After Christmas, Evanjelica sadly said her goodbyes to her friends and neighbors. Her older cousin, her grandaunt's eldest daughter, stayed with Adelina a few days, so Evanjelica felt a little more comfortable than if she were leaving her aunt completely alone.

Then seventeen-and-half-year-old Evanjelica got on a bus from Chaves to Lisbon, and then on a plane from Lisbon, Portugal to New York, USA. That was just the beginning of many more trips alone all around the world. Little did she know about her place or path on this life and that she was in the driver's seat the entire time.

She landed safely at John F. Kennedy Airport in New York on December 29, 1979, just in time to spend New Year's with her father and siblings. The day was a beautiful sunny day, yet she had many mixed feelings. For a young teen she had already been through so much, yet she didn't know what the future held for her. After New Year's, at the beginning of 1980, there were a few big blizzards, ice storms, and it was freezing cold. Evanjelica was not too happy because she had never seen so much snow and ice in her life. Her birth country had tropical weather. Yes, Portugal's winter was cold with a lot of frost and a little bit of snow, but it was bearable, not like a Connecticut winter. She told her father, "I want go back. I don't like this and I'm not staying here."

Ernesto countered, "Everybody adjusts, and you will too."

Her grandaunt Adelina died shortly after Evanjelica left Portugal, so she ended up staying in the US having a hard time adjusting to cold, freezing weather and to another new country. She entered the US with a green card and was legal to work. Two weeks after her arrival in mid-January 1980, one of her father's relatives got her a job in a factory, one mile from her father's house. Evanjelica was almost eighteen.

This job was making filters for fish aquariums and she was getting paid $2.50 hour in Bridgeport, Connecticut, where they lived. Evanjelica did overtime work and she made a decent paycheck. Every day she walked a mile to work and sometimes would get a ride from her coworkers.

IN THE USA, 1980

Evanjelica needed to save money to buy her first car and get her driver's license. She did not speak a word of English, and since she worked in the daytime, some her coworkers who had lived in the America longer told her she could attend night school to learn English.

She applied and went a few times with her two coworkers' friends. Her father found out and forbade from going to school. He said, "You are not going to school at age eighteen. You are too old and if you live under my roof, you obey my rules." The next day she told her friends she could no longer go to school because her father had forbidden it, and because she was in a new country, she couldn't risk being kicked out of his house.

Yet she knew she had to learn English in order to successfully live in this country. She had to find other ways to get her learning done. She saw this book at home from her younger stepsister who had come to the US when she was in grammar school. Evanjelica grabbed the book and read from the beginning to the end daily, and repeated it five times, until she understood the book and its meaning. She was never afraid of speaking; she wanted to learn at all costs, and she always asked questions.

Her father wanted her to take her driver's license so she could go grocery shopping and drive her stepmother around wherever she needed to go, as he didn't have time to drive her around. Evanjelica didn't know enough English yet to take the driver's test, and people at the DMV did not have a test in Portuguese at that time, only in English and Spanish. So, she decided to learn Spanish, which was easier. At the end of March 1980, she went for her driver's license and passed it the first time.

Once she had enough money saved after a year, she looked for a car and found a secondhand Ford Capri coupe, white with black stripes for $1000. She bought the vehicle and her responsibilities increased. After work she became a chauffeur to her stepmother and her daughters.

Evanjelica now had a driver's license and she improved her English every day by reading books and asking questions. She decided to improve her finances too to pay for gas, car insurance, and to pay her stepmother $50 week for food and board. After three months of working at this factory it closed down.

CHAPTER FIVE

LIFE IN THE UNITED STATES, 1980 TO 1985

Evanjelica switched to a factory that made leather jackets. Her pay was now $3.25 hour, but she did not have health insurance. She had worked there for almost a year. A few of her father's relatives, her second cousins, worked in the same factory with her, and because they had lived longer in the US, they had more experience with changing jobs to find better pay and benefits. Evanjelica asked them if she could use them as a reference when she applied for a new job.

She soon went to work for a pocketbook factory in Norwalk. Her relatives from her previous job were already working there a few months after she left the leather sportswear factory. Many of the women and men workers didn't drive on the highway since it was a long drive from Bridgeport to Norwalk. Some commuted on the company bus, but they didn't all fit on the bus; some had to get rides with people who drove to work.

Evanjelica slowly became more independent and adventurous and would drive her car from Bridgeport to Norwalk and give rides to those who didn't drive. She remembered when she was in the same situation of mercy of getting rides from others or walking to work. But the job was too far for anyone to walk.

After a year of working at the pocketbook factory and driving her car daily from Bridgeport to Norwalk, she saw a Dodge passenger van for sale. A coworker drove the van to work and it carried 15 people and they paid her for the ride. This woman was moving to Portugal and wanted to sell her van, and she thought about offering it to Evanjelica first since she worked at Norwalk and was not afraid to drive on the highway. It was old but selling for a reasonable price, so Evanjelica bought it. When the people at work saw her driving that big thing they offered to pay her $10 per week each instead of everybody getting rides individually. She ended up driving 15 people to work and made an extra $150 a week plus her paycheck; with all the overtime they worked from 7 a.m. to 7 p.m. She was making good money and had started a savings account. After three years of working for Norwalk, that same cousin who'd helped her out before moved to a company with more pay and better benefits.

Evanjelica was single, so she needed benefits, especially insurance. She got a job offer from an electronics factory. She put in her two weeks' notice at her old job, and sold her van to her godson's mother who had stayed at the pocketbook factory in Norwalk for many years because she didn't speak much English and was afraid of change.

Evanjelica was not afraid of change; she wanted to improve herself, improve her English, improve her income with a better paying job with better benefits. In the early months of 1984 at the electronics factory, she worked in production, and then six months later she learned that they needed an inspector. She applied and was told by management that it was an awfully hard job and a difficult position. Evanjelica asked, "Can I please try?" They gave her a chance to try the job with two weeks' training and then she needed to pass a test to fully earn that position. She learned the job and passed the test to become a quality assurance (QA) inspector.

Evanjelica had always been extremely ambitious since she was a little girl; she knew she wanted to have a lot of education and be someone important in life with a good career. Yet her life took different turns with her studies being interrupted with a war, a relocation to three different countries, and a negative, old-fashioned Portuguese father who did not support her educational goals. So, she had to find a way to work and put herself through school to get some sort of a career. She was now in her early twenties, a little more independent, and even if her father tried to throw her out of his house, she was making enough income to support herself. Evanjelica applied at the Institute of Beauty Academy to become a cosmetologist. She would work in the factory on the second shift and go to school during the day. It was going to be challenging with the language barrier since her English was still not too good, but she liked challenges and was willing to try and get better.

Chapter Six

Taking Chances, Cosmetology School 1984 to 1986

Evanjelica was taking a big risk applying for school at age 22, especially if her father thought 18 was too old to attend school, he would certainly not approve of her going to school at 22. It was also a big risk due to the language barrier. Would it be a waste of her money? Tuition was not cheap. Evanjelica knew she needed to try and reach her full potential. She wanted to be a good electronics inspector at the factory and be able to become a cosmetologist.

She thought to herself only time would tell if she would have a career or not. Even if she didn't pass the exam and didn't become a cosmetologist, this endeavor would never be a waste of time because her efforts would help improve her English. She never let go of hope. For Evanjelica, life was about taking chances and being willing to take a risk to achieve her dreams. She was determined to be a career woman, maybe not what she had in mind as a child when she wanted to be a scientist.

In every job, she was sharp and passed every test on the first try, yet she was not happy with herself. Before she started school she worked as a waitress part-time on weekends. She liked it but wanted to do more; she wanted a piece of paper, a license, she could hold as her career. A cosmetologist's license would be ideal so she could write her own ticket so she could enjoy her career, rather than be stuck in a factory. Yes, she had a good position as a QA inspector and it was going well, and since she worked second shift, she had free time during the day to do something with her life. The QA inspector position was good, but once she was out of the factory she was nothing.

Evanjelica started paying her tuition at the Institute of Beauty Academy. She had just enough money saved to pay half of the tuition, continue working, and then pay for the rest of her tuition monthly. She was excited with the idea of working with people, making them look and feel good. She would get up 6 a.m., shower, go to school at 8 a.m. to find parking, and then give herself an extra hour to study before class started at 9 a.m. until 1 in the afternoon. Then she'd go home, change from her uniform to normal clothing and go to work from 3:30 p.m. to 11:30 p.m., Monday to Friday. She would be in school a full day on Saturdays at the shop to put in her hours.

At school, like in any regular school, there was always one bad apple in the basket of ten good ones. Some students did not follow the rules.

Evanjelica and a few other girls from different countries, such as Cuba and Russia, were determined to finish their hours, graduate, and pass the exam. They all had a language barrier. Some American girls bullied them, made fun of them, saying, "Oh, we are Americans—we took that exam twice and we failed; it's a very difficult exam, so what makes you guys think you will pass? You don't even speak good English." Evanjelica and two other girls were concerned.

The secretary of the school overheard these conversations and noticed their concern. She called Evanjelica and the two non-American girls to her office and explained to them, "No worries about the exam," she said, "I know you guys will pass because, number one, you are paying your own tuition and that makes you more determined; number two, you obey the rules and follow instructions, you are hard workers, and I am confident that the three of you will pass the exam the first time. Your English will improve by the time you graduate and go for the exam. The only reason the other three failed their exams is because their parents are paying for their tuition, they do not work, they do not know value of the dollar—they are spoiled. So, do not let anything they say bother you; just do your work and focus on passing the exam."

Evanjelica worked a 40-hour full time job, the second shift from 3:30 to 11:30, went to school from 9 a.m. to 1 p.m., had a four-hour school day Monday to Friday, plus a full eight hours on Saturday—so 28 hours per week she put into school. She was young, healthy, and her ambition and determination gave her strength she needed. All she could think about was being a good inspector at work and passing her exam to get her license. She followed through on this routine from September 1984 to June 1986 and was on her way to completing 1500 hours in order to graduate, and then afterwards she would take the exam.

Her father and stepmother fussed about it, and when they found out, they gave Evanjelica a hard time and tried to stop her from going to school. At this point Evanjelica was already 22 years old and had gained some confidence and strength to stand up for her rights. Evanjelica told her father, "I have always obeyed your rules, and the only thing I want most in life is to have an education. I am not doing anything wrong in getting my education. I already paid for my tuition. I am sorry, but no, not this time, you can't stop me."

He replied, "Oh, your stepmother complains to me every day that you are never home to help her clean and do laundry. I am tired of listening to her; can you just take the time to help her?"

Evanjelica was really taking her biggest chance to stand up to her father as he was always so violent, then she remembered her grandaunt's words: "They cannot hurt you in the USA—it's not Africa. You are almost an adult and you can stand up to them."

She said to her father Ernesto, "What happened to Demonesa's daughters? Don't they all have hands? I have been their slave for many years since as a little girl when you took me away from my mom. And, yes, she is right I am never home. I work, I go to school. I do not dirty the house, I clean my room, I do my laundry, and everybody should do their own. Her daughters are still so young, yet they skip school to go out, be wild with boys and smoke and they get suspended. I am always doing your parenting job. I go to their school and talk to the principal on their behalf. Because you cannot take time out of work and do not speak English—that is your excuse—and you make me do your parenting job. Why can't you reprimand them? Or are you too afraid of my stepmother? They do whatever they want because they have their mother to protect them. Me, I have no mom to protect me, so I get yelled at for getting an education.

"You want to kick me out of your house and do as you please; the $75 per week I am paying you guys for food and board I can save and pay my own rent—I never eat at home anyway." Ernesto could not believe his daughter Evanjelica, who had always obeyed him, followed all the rules, was now no longer afraid of his threats.

As time passed, Evanjelica showed off different haircuts and styles from practicing on her classmates at school and them practicing on her. Her coworkers at the factory would ask her, "Oh, I like your haircut—can you give me a haircut like yours?" Because she was already busy during the week her coworkers would say, "Oh, what about Sunday?" So, on Sundays after Mass she would go to peoples' homes and give them haircuts; she was getting more experience and building up her clientele.

She was on her journey of a lifetime. Things were going in the right direction. At least for a while. She did not spend too much time at home and did not listen to her stepmother's complaints. Everything else was going well and she felt happy with her accomplishments.

Earlier in 1986 she got a little nervous because her senior year at school was hard, as she was getting ready to graduate and prepare for her exam. She worked extra hard, stayed up late after work to study, not getting much sleep; she started to feel weak, but she could not bear failing the exam.

In June 1986 she completed her 1500 hours, applied for her exam, paid the fee and waited to be called. Evanjelica passed the exam. She was overwhelmed and so happy—her hard work had paid off.

The owner of the school owned a few salons, and he liked

Evanjelica's qualifications. He asked her if she would like to work for one of his salons. Evanjelica accepted the offer, and reminded him of her schedule, her second shift job, and if it was okay with him if she could work for a few hours in the morning and on Saturday for a full day. "Great," he said. Evanjelica was filled with joy. She couldn't believe that she had not only passed the exam the first time; she also had a job offer from the most successful school and salon owner in town.

At the factory, she was getting more responsibilities, as all the inspectors had to do more and more training. She liked to challenge herself. She continued to work at the factory for benefits and it was good money. She also worked at the salon part-time and on Sundays she continued her home services to family, friends, and coworkers and was continuing to make and save a lot of money.

CHAPTER SEVEN

PORTUGAL SUMMER TRIP, 1986

After graduating from cosmetology school Evanjelica was 24 years old and had built up some vacation time at work. She planned a vacation to Portugal with her younger stepsister Zelda who wanted to go along. They went to the travel agency—in those days things were done more with pen and paper and not so much with technology—to book a flight from JFK Airport in New York to Porto, Portugal. Because it was summer Air Portugal and TWA were sold out, so they had to be put on the waiting list. The next day the travel agent called Evanjelica to tell her that there were only two seats available, but they would not fly straight into Portugal. Their flight would be on Iberia airlines from New York to Madrid, Spain, and then they would take a connecting flight from Madrid to Porto, Portugal via Air Portugal, which was the cheapest option since it was the Fourth of July. So, her father drove her and her sister to JFK Airport and saw them take off in the afternoon, as is typical with most international flights from the US to Europe to reach their destination in the early morning.

After an hour of being in the air, the captain announced, "Remain seated with your seat belts, we must turn around back to JFK. Prepare for an emergency landing." There was a leak in the aircraft and they were losing fuel. Passengers shouted, "Is there going to be an explosion?" and they started to scream and panic. The flight attendants tried to calm the passengers down speaking Spanish and English since Iberia was a Spanish airline. Zelda, who was 15 years old, cried, "I'm not going to see my mom and dad again. The plane is going to explode!"

Evanjelica had learned many good habits from her grandaunt that her stepmother and stepsisters didn't like, such as praying the Holy Rosary daily. Evanjelica not only prayed the Rosary daily, she prayed over all of her travels, driving or flying. And since she was fearless, she comforted her stepsister by holding her hand and saying, "Zelda, no it's not going to explode, we're going to be fine. But if it does explode it will be quick and we're not even going to feel it—it's out of our control."

Once Evanjelica was in her twenties she started to see life differently—que sera sera, whatever will be will be. She had become fearless and optimistic. The plane took a while to turn around and land, and once the aircraft hit the ground, the passengers got up ready to throw themselves out. Panic caused more problems because people were falling on top of each other and hurting themselves; it would have been best for everybody to just sit still and stay calm and focus. Back at JFK they waited for news and then were told that the aircraft had a major mechanical problem on one of its engines and couldn't reach its destination. Now the passengers would be transported to a hotel and leave the next day on a different plane. Because it was late, Evanjelica waited for the next morning to call her father and tell him about the incident.

He asked if Zelda was okay and Evanjelica replied, "Yes, we're all boarding in two hours on a different plane, same airline." Ernesto got very nervous and told Evanjelica, "Do not get on that plane. You and your sister need to stay at the airport and I'll go pick you guys up."

Evanjelica then said, "Well, our luggage is on the plane and if it was our destiny to die on that plane, it would had exploded and killed us yesterday when everyone was expecting it, but it didn't. We landed nicely and we are safe. And if our destiny is to die on this next plane so be it—it's out of our control."

Her father said, "If you want to go you go alone and leave your sister at the airport. I will go get her."

"Zelda is fifteen and I'm not leaving her at the airport alone." Then she asked her stepsister if she wanted to go with her on the flight or have her father come pick her up.

Zelda replied, "No, I want to go with you." Evanjelica had practically raised her two sisters Amaya and Zelda so they were closer to her then their own mother, Demonesa. Zelda told her father the plans and also said that she didn't want to spend her summer vacation at home listening to her mother's perpetual yelling.

They got on the shuttle back to airport and took off, landing in Madrid the next morning, but because they were a day late they lost their connections. So, they waited at the airport four hours for the next plane. Once in Porto, Evanjelica picked up a rental car and drove to Chaves. Since their vacation was cut short due to the airline issue, she could only stay in Chaves and in the Tras-os-Montes region a couple of days to visit her father's relatives and her grandaunt's children and grandchildren who were happy to see her again grown a little older than the last time.

Evanjelica and Zelda left Chaves after three days and they drove around to other cities: Algarve, Aveiro, Coimbra, Fatima, and Lisbon, of course, spending a day and night in each city, then they returned to the Porto airport to catch a flight to Madrid. They boarded the same airline, Iberia, where there was some issue taking off because the aircraft wouldn't lift from the ground. Finally, after a few tries it took off with a lot of turbulence. Most of passengers were complaining they would never travel on Iberia airlines again. Landing at JKF was surprisingly smooth. They were safely back on US ground. The two sisters had a great two weeks' vacation and Evanjelica returned Zelda safely to her father who was getting concerned about Evanjelica becoming too independent and fearless. He wanted to keep her under his control. But his little girl has grown up forcing herself to become independent so she could go back to her birth country and look for her family.

Evanjelica realized she had survived malaria at age 10 and survived war when a soldier had put a gun in her face at age 13. She had prayed for him to just pull the trigger and shoot her right there instead of taking her out of her father's car to go somewhere and rape her. Somehow the soldier changed his mind and walked away. Now, at age 24 she and sister had endured an emergency landing on a plane that should have crashed but did not.

She had told her father, "We do have a destiny. We don't know when or how we will go and have no control of it when our time comes. Yet we do have control of the choices we make."

Chapter Eight

Applying For US citizenship, the Trip to France, and the Proposal

Early in 1988 Evanjelica applied for her US citizenship because her English had greatly improved, and she thought it was time. She was told the process would take 18 months total.

She received some negative comments from family and coworkers who tried to discourage her. They told it was a very difficult test; they been in US longer than her and they had failed the test three times. What made her think she would pass it in such a short time of residency? Evanjelica told them, "I'm willing to try to see for myself how difficult it is."

She applied and waited to be called in. Meantime, she knew she had a few months, enough time to go on vacation to Portugal and use her saved days. She was still working full time in the factory and part time in the hair salon. Her father suggested she ship an old car he had in his driveway overseas, so she wouldn't have to rent a car in Portugal.

The travel agent told her it would take a month for the car to get to Portugal. The best option was to ship the car to France, where it would only take a week, and then fly in to Paris, so Evanjelica would pick up the car in France and drive it to Portugal. *Great, I'll get to see another country.* In mid-September 1988 she drove from Connecticut to New Jersey to ship the car, and then a week later she flew to Paris.

At first Ernesto was okay with his daughter going on this trip alone. He accepted that she was 26 years old, an adult and financially independent, not asking anyone for money, so she could go wherever she wanted to. But there was this guy who visited Ernesto's house often and was interested in Evanjelica, although Evanjelica didn't know this yet. He told Ernesto, "How can you allow your daughter, this young girl, to travel alone and drive from France to Portugal? I am a man and did that trip once. I swear I'll never to do it again. It's dangerous with a lot of deserts. She can get lost, kidnapped, even killed." After hearing this, Ernesto told Evanjelica she should cancel the trip because of what he heard; he didn't think it was safe for her to go.

Then Evanjelica answered her father, "I already shipped the car to France, and paid for my flight."

Ernesto answered, "You can cancel the flight and forget about car since it's old."

"No," she said. "I'm not going to ruin my plans just because some man is a chicken and afraid of challenges. I'd like to do this trip and see for myself how dangerous or difficult it really is."

Her flight day approached; Ernesto drove his daughter to Newark International Airport in New Jersey. During their trip from Shelton, Connecticut, to New Jersey, Evanjelica told her father, "No worries, I will call you as soon I land in Paris, and during my drive from France to Portugal, I'll make sure not to drive too late at night, and follow the directions to get to Portugal and back to the US safe. I know you're concerned about my safety; you are a parent and I thank you. But I am now a 26-year-old adult and responsible for all my actions. My grand-aunt Adelina taught me about choices and consequences. I will take the proper precautions, so be at peace."

After hearing this Ernesto knew his daughter was no longer his little girl, that she never really had a chance to be a little girl. She matured at a very young age, with a heavy load on her shoulders, and had the total responsibility of taking care of her siblings. Now she was just getting stronger and more independent.

Ernesto started to tell his daughter about this guy who visited his house often. The reason why he didn't want Evanjelica to go on this trip was because the man was interested in her.

Ernesto continued, "This guy is married, and his wife is in Portugal. He came to the US on a visiting visa and wants to marry a woman living here so he can stay. He is willing to pay $10,000. That's a lot of money, so I told him I would talk to my oldest daughter saying, 'It's time for you to get married; all of your younger siblings are married except you.'"

Evanjelica grew terribly angry at her father. "Really, Dad? Are you serious? I just applied for my US citizenship. I would never break the law; besides, he is married, and I would never break a marriage, destroy a family, and I'm not attracted to him. I do not care how much money he is offering. I am making enough on my own and don't need his money. It's about doing the right thing. I cannot believe you as my father agreed with this stranger about marrying me without my consent." She pointed her finger at her father. "If you are desperate to help this guy, remember your two daughters left your house with drug addicts. You forbade me from getting an education while my sisters had the freedom to go school, yet they dropped out to be with guys. Maya is married to a man who doesn't work; she is suffering financially. And Zelda is living with a guy much younger than her. He is irresponsible and all he does is smoke and drink. My sisters are struggling, and they can use the $10,000. Have them marry the guy so they can have the money."

Ernesto replied, "He wants you, not your sisters."

"He's not going to have me. If he is married and just wants to stay here, he's not going to live with a woman who marries him. It's just business, so it doesn't matter who that woman is. It certainly won't be me. I know a lot people do these kinds of marriages; I consider them illegal. I know I'm not like a lot of people. I'm me and don't like to be pressured into things I disapprove of."

They arrived at Newark Airport; Ernesto hugged and kissed his daughter and wished her a safe trip. Evanjelica told her father, "I love you, Dad. I'll call you as soon I land in Paris and throughout the trip." She flew overnight to Paris, then took the train from Paris to Le Havre harbor and picked up the car. She would start her journey the next day since she would be on the road all day and needed to rest.

After she picked up the car it was already getting dark, so she looked for hotel in Le Havre. In a strange country she didn't want chance driving at night and had promised her father she wouldn't. After arriving at the hotel, she called her father and updated him on her travel plans.

For the next week she explored France, spending two days on a beautiful pilgrimage to the Lady of Lourdes shrine in Lourdes, visiting the grotto, seeing the movie, *The Song of Bernadette,* as well as seeing Saint Bernadette's parents' house. Evanjelica spent one day in Bordeaux and then only stayed two days in Spain, and then she stayed three weeks in Portugal.

She then visited relatives and her old coworker Odette and her husband Mateus and son Nick who used to live in the US, but moved to Portugal a few years before. Evanjelica worked with Odette in the factory for a couple years, and she didn't know why Odette and her husband only lived in the US for five years. Evanjelica found out many years later that this couple had done some illegal activity and had stolen money from the company and were deported. They used that money in Portugal to build their house and business. Odette's uncle was the architect building her house and had a few young men working for him.

Odette introduced Evanjelica to a few of the guys, including this young man, Asmodeus, one of her uncle's employees. Evanjelica was always nervous about meeting men due to the trauma of her father being abusive to her mom. She never went on dates until she was introduced to Asmodeus. He was good looking and appeared hardworking, but she knew nothing about him, except for what her friend Odette told her. Evanjelica asked Odette if perhaps he was just interested in her because she was American. She knew America was a big illusion for a lot Portuguese people. But Evanjelica only wanted to date and marry a man for love, not for convenience.

Odette told Evanjelica, "I'll put my hands on fire for him." When Evanjelica heard this, she trusted her friend Odette, who really did not know much about Asmodeus either, or she would never have assured Evanjelica that he was good guy when she herself didn't know him that well; she just went by what her uncle told her. Little did she suspect that Odette's uncle wanted to help Asmodeus get out of Portugal to find a better life. Evanjelica was for a good target since she was single, made good money, and did not know she was being used.

And Evanjelica did not know Odette was not an honest person either. When they worked together in America Odette seemed like a good person. Evanjelica found out the hard and painful way many years later who Odette really was.

Odette told Evanjelica, "You helped me a lot back in the US, and now I want to return the favor. I know you are staying at a hotel, but come stay at my house to help me with my store." As Evanjelica helped Odette daily at her mini market, more guys were showing interest in her. She knew the interest was not about her but about them coming to America. Since Evanjelica was staying at her house, Odette planned a double date for herself and Mateus, inviting Asmodeus to help start the conversation with the shy Evanjelica. Yes, she was young, naïve, and trusted her so-called friend Odette. She did not know she was about to enter a very dark and painful path of her life.

In mid-October, after a week of being in Portugal, Ernesto called Evanjelica to let her know she had mail from Immigration. She asked her father to open it and see what it said. He told her the exam was on November 4, o she cut her vacation short by a week. She came back to the US to take the test, which she passed.

Now she needed to wait six to eight months to be sworn in as an American citizen.

She wrote a letter to Odette and to Asmodeus that she had arrived back home safely. Asmodeus replied back. From his letters she could tell that he didn't have much education. Although he didn't write very well, they were very romantic letters; she started to like him. He was good looking, hardworking, and romantic. Odette also assured her he was honest. Evanjelica was willing to give him a chance.

Things started to happen fast. After communicating by mail, they talked by phone, and nine months later he proposed.

THE BEGINNING OF HER DARK LIFE STARTS...

While Evanjelica was working two jobs at the hair salon and factory, she also started planning her wedding which took place in Portugal. Planning a wedding is stressful and having it take place in a different country is twice more complicated. She also needed to prepare all the documentation necessary to bring her new husband to the States. while still waiting to get sworn in as an American citizen. She had to be a citizen to bring him over; otherwise, she would have to wait for him an additional two years.

Once she knew the day of the swearing-in ceremony was June 2, 1989, she set the date for their wedding as June 17, 1989. Like any young girl she thought this was her fairy tale and her happily-ever-after.

Evanjelica went to the Portuguese Embassy in the US and spoke to the Portuguese Consulate, who prepared all documents necessary for her spouse's petition. The Consulate advised her to wait for the swearing-in to receive the American citizen papers and passport so she could bring her future spouse with her. They also asked her to take her flight tickets with her on the day of the swearing-in so they could speed up the passport process.

On June 2, 1989, she went to the Bridgeport, Connecticut court as scheduled for the American citizen swearing-in ceremony where there were three hundred other people there. Everything went well and they told her that her passport would arrive in two or three weeks. Evanjelica anxiously presented her airline tickets because she only had few days before she left the US and needed that passport. The officer gave her a location in Stamford where she could go in person to pick up her passport, and two days later she had it in hand, now ready to fly to Portugal on June 8th. She was happy, excited, and like any normal bride, nervous.

Chapter Nine

The Wedding

Long-distance relationships are hard because we don't get to see our partner's qualities, personality, behavior, and temper. In his letters Asmodeus seemed to have good intentions. But later in life after being married for a while, Evanjelica noticed Asmodeus was not romantic at all. She questioned him why he was romantic in his letters and not in person, and he replied he never wrote any of letters to Evanjelica; his old girlfriend Orusula wrote them for him. He didn't know how to write, and he wanted to impress Evanjelica. Well, obviously Orusula didn't write well either. Evanjelica was devastated to find out she'd been used and abused.

During those nine months of their long-distance relationship, Evanjelica was busy working full time on the swing shift at the factory in QA inspection, part time at the salon, plus planning her wedding and preparing all documents necessary to bring to her spouse. She looked forward to whatever future possibilities would come into her life; she would handle them when crossing that bridge.

Just about two months before she planned to leave on her flight to Portugal for the wedding, she had a horrifying dream. She was trying on her white wedding gown and when she got in front of the mirror she saw her gown transform from white into pitch black. She woke up to realize she had not yet bought her gown in real life—why was she having that kind of dream when she had never tried on a gown? She was so bothered by it she told her father about the dream. He said, "Oh, you won't be staying married too long to your husband. He will die shortly after the wedding."

"Don't say that," said Evanjelica. "I don't want to be a widow right after I get married!" She was troubled by this dream. Later in life she found out the reason her dream gown changed from white to black; it didn't mean she would be a widow, yet it was a sign. A black dress meant a dark painful marriage, based on lies, cheating, dishonesty, and disrespect. The sad part is that she fell in love with the wrong man whom she thought was going to be her world, her life partner. He turned out to be just a liar using her as a bridge to come to America for a better life for himself.

After that dream Evanjelica was afraid of buying a wedding gown and trying it on; she was deeply troubled. She needed to shop for a gown because time was growing short with the wedding date quickly approaching. So, off she went to the first bridal store on her list. She then saw all the dresses were black; she ran out of the store and got into her car thinking maybe she should call off the wedding. It would be less painful than face her husband's death right after the wedding. Evanjelica was confused, not knowing what to do.

A week went by and that following Sunday she went back to a store, this time not a bridal store, but a regular clothing store. For a person who didn't like to spend time in stores, Evanjelica was now spending all day in this store just trying on all kinds of dresses—she needed to face her fear. She did not buy a dress, but she did leave from that store feeling better—confident and not afraid.

She finally found a wedding gown, and needed to assure herself she had all the right documents necessary to get married and bring her spouse to the States. She also had to fully furnish her apartment and purchase a second vehicle, a used car, for her husband before she left for Portugal.

The day of the flight approached as her father and stepmother went to Portugal since no one else in the family was able to go. Ernesto told his daughter he couldn't pay for her wedding due to being laid off. Evanjelica told her father, "It's okay, I was not expecting for you to pay." She had saved enough to pay for her wedding and just enough for a party in America after the wedding to introduce everyone to her new husband. Ernesto told Evanjelica he would pay for the party, but when the time came he refused to pay, so Evanjelica ended up paying for that event, plus the wedding, her husband's documents, and the airfare tickets.

After flying to Portugal, Asmodeus was in Lisbon waiting for them. They got married in Chaves, Portugal, June 1989, and the day after the wedding the couple drove to Lisbon to the American Embassy to introduce him as her new spouse and prepare his petition. It took two weeks for Asmodeus to get approved because July and August was tourist time in Portugal, and so they had to be put on a waiting list.

On August 17 they finally got a flight to come to the US. Evanjelica was 27 years old, naïve, innocent, and in love. Little did she know that her wedding was not fairy tale, but a beginning of a painful nightmare. She did not know his intentions of landing a better life to impress his old girlfriend who dumped him nine years prior because he was poor.

Back in the US After the Wedding, 1989

Once established in their apartment, Asmodeus criticized Evanjelica on the furniture, and for buying him a used car. He had his illusions of coming to America and somehow thought he had married a rich woman. Evanjelica immediately clarified things for him, and said, "I don't know where you got that idea that I was rich—I never told you that I was rich."

He replied, "Well, I just imagined you were rich because you live in America."

She felt insulted, and told him, "I wish you would have had this conversation with me before the wedding. I would have changed my mind. It's too late now, we're already married. I never told you or anybody I was rich. I was refugee of war, had to leave my country for two different countries, and for 10 years I lived in US before I married you. I worked hard for my money. I paid for our wedding in Portugal and for your trip here. I paid for the welcoming party not because I am rich, but because I had no choice. My father told me he would not pay for my wedding. Your family did not pay either. They did not even give any gifts. I understand now they thought I was rich. My furniture is brand new and I like it."

She paused to take a long breath. "I don't see any reason why you are criticizing me knowing where you came from. I did not criticize your family's house which was dirty with old broken furniture. The vehicle I bought for you is a Peugeot. It's not new, but it's newer than my Mazda. It's what I could afford. I might not be rich, yet I'm giving you everything you imagined you would have. To a lot of Portuguese people, coming to America is a big illusion. They think money falls from the trees. You're lucky you married a woman who made your life easy, brought you to America for a better life. You have a car to drive and house to live in. I wish I was that lucky. You see, when I came to the United States, it was wintertime and so cold. Every day I walked a mile to work until I saved enough money to buy my first car, and it was a used vehicle. I always buy used cars as long they run and I'm grateful for it. Sometimes I would get a ride from coworkers, and for the most part I walked. My life was not as easy as I am making yours. Nobody ever gave me anything."

After that conversation, Asmodeus, who was youngest of nine siblings and a stubborn man who always got his way, started to give his wife Evanjelica a hard time. He didn't speak to her for a full week so he could get what he wanted. They were newlyweds and Evanjelica could not comprehend his behavior. *What did she do wrong?*

One Sunday Evanjelica was home alone and bothered with her husband's behavior. So, she called Odette in Portugal who introduced them. Evanjelica explained to Odette it looked like Asmodeus did not marry her for love. "Why did he want to come to the United States? He expected me to have a new car for him, and he criticized my furniture. I wish I could give him better things, but I don't have it. I did what I could afford; I spent a lot money going overseas to get married plus all documents to bring him, and a welcoming party here to introduce him to my relatives."

Odette told Evanjelica, "I am sorry I introduced you to him, and assured you he was good guy, that I would put my hands on fire for him. You trusted me and we are friends. But I really did not know him that well."

Odette continued. "I have a confession to make. I never met his family and only saw him while he worked here. Last year when you came to visit me, he told my uncle he was interested in you but was too shy to ask you out because you were American. That's why I planned the double date, so you guys could start talking. You were both adults and I know the type of woman you are. You're a hard-working woman and wanted a hard-working man. I thought the two of you would make a good couple. And it would be nice to take him out of this small town into a country where he could have better opportunities.

"People that come shopping to my mini market tell me his family are not good people, that they are trouble. I feel terrible knowing you married a man you did not know well."

Evanjelica told Odette, "I wish you'd given me this information before I married him. I mean, he is a good-looking and hard-working man. I was attracted to him, but was also concerned that he might just want to come to America. When you told me would put your hands on fire for him I felt comfortable to continue the relationship. And my gut feeling was right—he just wanted a better life. I don't think he loves me.

"I'm Catholic and had to have a religious wedding. I do not believe in divorce; I just must make the best of it. I hope he does not become abusive like my father was with my mother. I will then break my vows."

Odette agreed and told Evanjelica, "Good for you, I would do the same. If my husband ever hits me I'll leave him. Best of luck and try your best to make it work." They said goodbye.

As soon as Asmodeus found himself married and secure in the US, he immediately started to mess with Evanjelica's head. His purpose was to drive her insane. He would misplace things and blame her for it. Many times, she witnessed him putting items down on the living room table and then when she walked to the kitchen he would come up behind her and ask, "Where is the hammer?"

"What hammer?"

"The hammer that I just placed on the kitchen table."

She would answer him, "I just saw you putting it on the living room table."

And right away he would insult her saying that something was wrong with her mind, that she was so crazy, and ask, "why am I married to a crazy woman like you?" She would reply, "I'm not crazy and I did not touch your hammer. I had no need to. I saw you putting it down on the coffee table when you sat on the sofa to take your shoes off. Your shoes and hammer are still in the same place. I never touched them. If you regret marrying a crazy woman like me then pay me back every penny I spent on you and go back to Portugal." Every time she threatened to send him back to Portugal and demanded him to refund her of every penny, he would behave for a few months. Asmodeus was an ignorant man and not good in school, yet evil smart. Like a snake he knew how to manipulate the system in his soft-spoken way with people, then spit out his poison. He knew how to convince people to believe him; some did believe him, but not all. The only reason people respected him was because he was married to Evanjelica, a well-respected woman. Evanjelica did not bow down to him and that irritated him.

He knew that his wife Evanjelica brought him to the US with a green card. He was a legal alien and from what he'd heard at the US Embassy in Portugal for up to two years she had right to throw him out of the country and back to Portugal if he did not behave. So, he knew when and how much he could push her buttons. This was a man that everybody liked because he was hard working and soft spoken. Nobody knew his true colors as he would smile, but behind their backs he would criticize people. He was liar and a backstabber. It was what he did best: criticize people who helped him, but at the same time know how to put on a fake smile.

This upset Evanjelica deeply since she was straightforward with people. She read the truth on people's faces and expected the same in return. Unfortunately, that did not work in her favor because many people choose to be surrounded with lies and fake friends, rather than to believe in the truth. Evanjelica chose her friends wisely and wanted her friends to be loyal and trustworthy. *Always tell me the truth to my face. I am big girl and can handle it.*

Asmodeus thought people were just like him, and somehow he felt supported enough to start insulting his wife in public, and in front of her own family. Just because she did not defend herself in public did not mean she approved of his behavior or was afraid of him; she was polite and did not want to cause a scene. So, every time they were out at gatherings with family and friends Evanjelica was not able to ever say a word until this time.

At this gathering Asmodeus told her, "Shut up, you're crazy and stupid. Nothing coming out of your mouth is right, so shut it!" Then he also accused her of sleeping with her hairstyling clients, a claim he had made several times before. Somehow he felt himself supported because a lot people liked him, and nobody would say anything to protect Evanjelica. This gave him a lot of power over her, and people didn't say anything because it was not their business to interfere in a couple's life; they waited for Evanjelica to defend herself which she never did. She would always try to handle the issue at home, but this was a mistake because her family and friends did not know what happened at home between the two of them.

Unfortunately, not speaking up did not work in her favor. Many felt threatened by her strong personality and this led people to believe she was at fault, but they soon learned the truth. Truth might take a long time, sometimes even years, yet it always comes out. Her entire life, since she was a little girl, she held herself apart from bad influences. She'd rather be alone without friends, than surround herself with corrupt influences. *In the world we live in, it's easy for people to believe in a liar.*

Asmodeus would go cry "victim" the next day that she was abusing him and that she destroyed his life by bringing him to US since he had no family here. "It's really hard to live with a woman like her." Some of her family members did not believe him and knew how he insulted her. He would cry fake tears and some people believed him and would start to question her over why she was abusing her husband. They wondered if the rumors were true: was she cheating on her husband with her hairstyling clients like he claimed?

Evanjelica was shocked by what she'd just heard come out of Asmodeus's mouth and replied, "First of all, my marriage problems are none of my family's or anybody's concern. I do not think you know me at all, because if you did you would not believe the lies you hear about me. I am a professional and don't get romantically involved with clients, and, yes, I do give men haircuts—I always have, it's my job. I'm unisex cosmetologist; my husband knew that when I gave him, all his brothers, nephews, nieces, and sisters haircuts two days before our wedding. Why didn't he say something about it then? I would have reconsidered marrying him.

"Second of all that is incorrect. First he accuses me of cheating because men at church look at me. I don't notice anybody looking at me. I go to church to thank the Lord for my blessings, not to pay attention to who is looking at me. People are free to look and that does not mean anything; it doesn't mean I'm cheating. Insecure people are normally the ones cheating, like my father did with my mother, a perfect example. I know my place as a married woman. Now he is accusing me that I am abusing him. How so? He is the one who is always throwing insults at me. Quite frankly I am getting tired of his insults and ingratitude. If people are that ignorant to believe his lies and judge me without hearing my side of story, without investigating the truth, so be it. I have no control over people's behavior and who they should believe.

"But I do have control of my life and my marriage. I do not interfere in anybody's marriage and I would appreciate it if my marriage and private life would not be invaded by weak-minded people. You are my family. You've known me longer than you've known him. If you want to judge me learn the facts first." Evanjelica did not care if those family members were ever going to speak to her again. She had set them straight and her life and marriage were none of their concern.

They eventually realized Evanjelica was right and in a few years she pulled herself away from all her relatives and all the negativity.

Chapter Ten

Pregnancy and Birth of Evanjelica's First-born Son

Evanjelica continued to work as electronics inspector full time and because she was now married she switched to the day shift and worked at the hair salon only on Saturdays. Three months after being back from Portugal, she started to feel sick. This was puzzling since she had never felt nauseated. She felt dizzy, had strong headaches, and was losing her balance. She was not sure if it was because of the trip overseas or from working with a lot of chemicals. She went to the doctor and left with good news. She was pregnant. But it was a risky pregnancy; she was happy she was going to be a mom, yet concerned she had to take precautions.

She continued her normal life of working and caring for the house and husband. She visited the doctor frequently and had to be admitted to the hospital several times during the pregnancy due to complications. The doctor finally told her to stop working and be on full bed rest. It was hard for Evanjelica to be on bed rest since she was always energetic and super active, but she would sacrifice anything to save her baby. Two weeks before the due date she had a doctor's appointment and was rushed to the hospital, and that same day she started having heavy contractions, and then had to have an epidural. After 20 hours of contractions, the baby's heartbeat stopped; she was nervous and thought she had lost the baby. She needed an emergency C-section to save the baby and the doctor wanted to give her anesthesia, yet she wanted to stay awake to see her baby being born. She had already lost hope.

In the early morning hours of June 1990, her baby boy was born. He didn't cry, so Evanjelica thought maybe she had lost him. The doctors who were trying to save the baby took him with them while they spoke with her. Finally, after an hour the pediatrician came to talk to her, and as he approached her she asked him, "Did I lose my baby?"

He replied, "No, we saved him. Congratulations, you have a beautiful baby boy." Then the nurse quickly showed her the baby and rushed him to further treatment. At 8 a.m., still drowsy from the epidural, Evanjelica finally met her first-born son and held him in her arms. She inspected her baby to assure he was okay and had ten fingers and ten toes. "He is very bruised from the hard labor," the nurse said, "but it will clear up in a couple of days."

Holding her baby was a special moment, a very happy feeling. Evanjelica and her baby Rafael stayed in the hospital over a week. Back at home her house was a mess, with the sink full of dirty dishes and dirty laundry; Asmodeus never helped Evanjelica with the house chores. So, she put the baby in his crib and started cleaning the house even though she had undergone surgery and could not do much bending. Since she'd started her maternity leave a month before giving birth she was due back to work in three weeks. Fortunately, Evanjelica had one retired trustworthy friend living near her house who could babysit Baby Rafael since her family all worked and lived far way. The first week she cried every day driving to work being apart from her baby and could not wait to get out of work to hold him again.

After work she would pick up the baby from the babysitter and go home to bathe him, feed him, and put him his crib, and start cooking dinner. Asmodeus worked construction and came home two hours later than her so she would have dinner ready when he got home. After dinner they would sit in the living room to watch TV, and she would hold the baby and play with him.

She then noticed a change in her husband—that he did not want her to play with the baby or even hold the baby to hug and kiss him. Asmodeus would give his wife weird looks, and make comments like, "Why are you always holding the baby? You're going to spoil him."

She would tell him, "I do not always hold him. I worked all day and came home and cooked dinner and now I'm just holding him. I missed him all day." Asmodeus did that quite often. Evanjelica got concerned one day, so she talked to her best friend about the comments her husband made when she held the baby. Her friend, who was older with a lot more experience, told her he was jealous. "That's ridiculous," said Evanjelica. "He is his son and looks just like him."

"Yes," she replied, "but the baby is now taking attention away from him; believe me, I know of a lot of men who get jealous of babies and it actually causes a lot of divorces."

"That is extremely sick," Evanjelica said. "I give him attention too, though the baby needs me more." One summer day, when Rafael was three months old, Evanjelica invited her father, stepmother, her uncle Bernardino (her father's younger brother who made the petition for all of them to come to US), and her aunt Paula over to have a barbecue at her house. Evanjelica had a close relationship with her uncle and aunt and was appreciative for all they had done for her. The barbecue was a small token of gratitude since her uncle always invited them to his house for gatherings and parties.

Evanjelica's father, because he was also abusive to her mom, had a weak mind, of course, and was a quick believer who supported his son-in-law a few times on his lies. He told him he would talk to his daughter, giving Asmodeus more power to abuse Evanjelica.

On the day of the barbecue, Asmodeus felt supported and decided to snap at his wife once again in front of her family to humiliate her. She had gotten up early to bathe and feed the baby, put him on a bouncing chair in front of the TV so she could keep eye on him while preparing the meal for the barbecue. Asmodeus never helped her around the kitchen or with the baby. He never changed a diaper; he would play with the baby, but if he cried or needed changing, he would call his wife. Evanjelica didn't bother asking Asmodeus for any help in the kitchen, especially after he refused to pitch in the day of the barbecue. She tried her best to get the house clean and the food ready, and to get everything done before the guests arrived. As everybody was eating and talking, Asmodeus decided to humiliate his wife once again in front of her family. Yet because some weak-minded people believed him and supported his lies didn't mean everyone was on the same page. He was in for a big surprise.

Asmodeus brought up an argument he'd had with his wife earlier that month when he told her, "Tomorrow I'm going to work in Danber." Evanjelica had asked him, "Denver, Colorado?" He replied, "No, Danber, Connecticut." She told him, "I'm sorry, I've been in the USA for ten years, but I don't think there is a Danber in Connecticut; maybe you mean Danbury?" He started arguing with her. "Oh, Santiago, the guy who got me the job, lives in America for thirty years, a lot longer than you and that's what he told me. What makes you think you know more than him?" She told him, "I don't know more than anyone, but maybe you just misunderstood him, or he spelled it incorrectly. I believe he meant Danbury." Asmodeus would not stop arguing and calling his wife stupid, telling her she just wanted to be the center of attention trying to know more than anyone.

Evanjelica was correct, and she knew how stubborn her husband was, never admitting to being wrong. She then told him, "Never mind, it's pointless arguing with you." And she let the matter go. But he bought up that subject again the day of barbecue to embarrass her that he was right because she had let it go. Everybody was quiet and the conversation paused for a moment. Then when her uncle Bernardino looked at her with a mean look, she thought her uncle was going to yell at her, yet to her surprise Bernardino turned around to Asmodeus and told him:

"I am tired of seeing you insult my niece; you did it several times while in my house. Now for everything I just heard you saying, it appears my niece is correct. The correct word is Danbury not Danber. A lot of Portuguese people speak slang

English including Santiago and other people you are working with you. Just because they've lived in the US longer than my niece doesn't necessarily mean they know more than her. Evanjelica speaks better English than a lot of people living here longer than her. And," Bernardino continued, "as far as you complaining you're working too hard and that she's trying to make you into a slave because she politely asked you to help her in the kitchen, she works hard too; since she came to the US she has worked two jobs, or a full-time job and school. She continues to work harder than any woman I've ever seen. She's now taking care of a newborn baby, working a full-time job, and caring for the house—that's not hard work to you? I know you work in construction and that is hard work, but you come home, take a shower, eat and sit on the sofa, watch TV, and then your job is done. Evanjelica's job is never done. She works a full-time job at the factory, and part time at the hair salon on Saturday and then comes home and takes care of the baby, house, family; her work does not end until she goes to bed and then she wakes up to start all over again.

"She picks up the baby at the babysitter. You could do that on your way home from work, and she can come straight home to prepare the meals. So if she asks her husband to help her with the house chores, it is not treating you as a slave; it is working together as a couple."

Asmodeus was not happy that someone had finally stood up for his wife. He had to think of ways to circumvent this and slowly make people turn against her, but never her uncle and aunt. They liked Asmodeus in the beginning and shortly saw he had issues.

They continued conversing with him but never supported his behavior towards their niece. He tried turning her against her uncle and aunt by bringing lies to Evanjelica like, "Bernardino and his wife told me, 'oh my niece doesn't deserve a good guy like you.'"

Evanjelica told Asmodeus, "I know it's not true. I know my uncle Bernardino and my aunt Paula well and they know me well too. I only believe in things told right to my face, so unless I hear from them then I don't believe you."

Every time she tried to teach him to help better himself he would insult her by saying she was trying to be the center of attention and thought she knew it all. It was hard to understand this man who refused to learn and was jealous of people who were more successful than him.

Chapter Eleven

Relocation Plans Back to Portugal, 1991

Time passed and Asmodeus started more drama between his wife and her family. He was working on his Plan B to convince Evanjelica to move to Portugal so he could control her with the support of his family and secure her money and everything she owned on his home turf. He was not book smart, but he knew how to manipulate people to get what he wanted. He entered their marriage with a lie, fathered a baby with his old girlfriend, and then used Evanjelica as a bridge to a better life. He needed to find ways to get out of his marriage with a clean face, so he tried to drive Evanjelica insane and make her believe she was crazy so he'd have reason to divorce her. He was able to take everything from her such as her money and material things, but not her sanity.

He gave his wife a hard time complaining daily how she'd destroyed his life by bringing him to the US and that he should have stayed in Portugal with his family. He did not like America. Evanjelica tried comforting her husband and told him, "You will get used to it. I did not like it either at first, just give it some time."

"Oh I knew it," he replied, "You just want me to stay here and be a slave to your father, your uncle, and Santiago at work who keeps telling me he's going to retire and move to Portugal and give me his house, but he never does. I do all the work while Santiago just sits on a machine."

She answered him, "You knew what my life was like in the United States, and if you didn't want to leave your family then you should had stayed single or married someone else. I would have saved myself a lot of money and work on all those documents. To Santiago, the only thing you should have to say about him is to get on your knees and thank him for getting your good-paying job; be thankful for the blessings people bring to you. Regarding my father and uncle, they never treated you as a slave; they never asked you for anything. You volunteer to go help them every Sunday as an excuse to not attend Mass with me because the men at church look at me. Number one: you should go to church and thank the Lord for your blessings, not wonder if some man is looking at your wife. Number two: since you volunteer to help both my father and my uncle they accepted your offer mostly to help us with money because we are newlyweds. They fed you and paid you $100 each day. How is that treating you like a slave? You have no idea what a life of slavery is. See, when my father took me from my mom to live with him, my stepmother put me to hard work. At age eight I had to clean the house, cook, wash the laundry tank—there was no washer in those days—hang the clothes and iron them when all of them were dry.

"Many times, my stepmother would lock me and my brothers in a dark room all day without food. My father was out traveling so she did whatever she pleased, and when my father returned home from his trips she would lie to him so he could beat us. That's more like slavery to me than what you are describing, which is volunteering to help when they feed and pay you. Only spoiled crybabies would complain of such things. I feel blessed and appreciative when people feed me and pay me for whatever work I do for them."

Things started to get very tense between the couple as Asmodeus kept putting pressure on Evanjelica to move back to Portugal. She told him her life was here in the United States and that she did not have anybody in Portugal. He replied, "You have me. I am your husband and you're supposed to follow me wherever I go." In order to please her husband and try to save her marriage she agreed to move to Portugal with him. Yet she did not know his true intentions.

In November of 1991 they got a call from the International Red Cross. Evanjelica's younger brother Gabriel who was raised by their mom (she had lost contact with both her mother and brother for 18 years) was a sergeant in the Air Force and stationed in Ota-Alenquer, Portugal, for a few months and was looking for his father Ernesto, his brother Agostinho, and sister Evanjelica. He said he had only a couple months left in Portugal, and then had to return to Angola with the military, so, Evanjelica told him, "Since we were already planning to move to Portugal we can just go a few months earlier because I want to see you."

Evanjelica and her son little Rafael were Americans, but they needed to have dual citizenship in order to live in Portugal more than 60 days without penalties. Before they left for Portugal, Evanjelica went to the Portuguese Consulate and told them her emergency situation—that she needed to go to Portugal immediately and needed her documents prepared ASAP. As her papers were being processed, she ordered a 43-foot container to ship her furniture and car from the US to Portugal. The consulate got the documents ready within 10 days and advised Evanjelica to board at JFK to leave the US with a US passport and enter Portugal with a Portuguese passport. It would make it easier for both her and her son, and to pick up the container and register a car in Portugal since everything was in her name.

Chapter Twelve

The Reunion with Brother and Mom, Missing For 18 Years, 1992

Evanjelica booked three airfare tickets for herself, her husband, and her son Rafael, now 18 months old. They flew to Lisbon where her brother Gabriel was waiting at the airport with a man and woman from the International Red Cross. Meeting her brother after 18 years of being lost from each other was emotional, and she was overwhelmed. So many tears. They had so much to talk about.

Evanjelica, her son Rafael, and husband Asmodeus stayed at the hotel in Alenquer for a few days while visiting with her brother, and she would go to the air force base during the day to be with him. She asked Gabriel if their mom was still living, and he said yes, and he arranged for them to talk on the phone. Evanjelica was proud of her brother being a sergeant in the air force, and a HERO who'd found his family. As they conversed, Gabriel told his older sister of his experiences back in Angola growing up with a rifle on his hands, learning to use it on his own to protect himself, his mother, and his siblings, and then soon after joining the military and making sergeant in the air force at an early age.

Evanjelica told her brother, "I'm proud of you. You're my hero, brother, and Jesus watches over you. I'm glad you're here alive and safe. And I'm glad you found us. See, our father and stepmother lied to everyone that you guys were dead. When I became aware of what was being said I confronted our father, and after that he and our stepmother started criticizing and degrading our mother among his relatives, telling everyone that our mother was crazy and that's why he left her. I corrected that notion and told people that's not true. My mother left him because of his infidelity I remember well; I was six years old and would never forget that day and all the pain that came with it.

"Our mom raised you guys alone in a country with an active war and you're now a man of honor with a good position. Our father and stepmother raised their kids in America, the land of opportunity. I don't know what the future holds for them, but as of now it has been nothing but embarrassment. Our stepmother's older son Alessandro is not our father's son. I found out she became pregnant by another man when our father got involved with her. She is always making a jealous scene over Mom. Remember, our father cheated on Mom while she was pregnant and was with a woman who was pregnant with another man's child. So, her son Alessandro is in big trouble in the United States. He was screwing Cabo Verdean married women, not just one but several. Their husbands beat him up and almost killed him. Alessandro ran away from Connecticut to Florida. Our stepmother's two daughters, Zelda and Maya, ran out of the house at age 16 with drug addicts, yet our stepmother has a lot of nerve to even open her mouth to criticize Mom, a better woman than her."

Evanjelica continued. "I'm hoping her children will amend their lives and have a good future. I was their slave all these years. I wanted so badly to go back to Angola to look for you guys, but our father discouraged me from going. He assured me you were dead and for many years I struggled with feeling something deep within my heart that told me you guys were still alive. When I got married two years ago the first thing I told my husband was that I wanted to go to Angola to look for you guys. I wanted him as a man to accompany me. First he told me he would go with me, but a lot of things have changed. It is my dream to visit my birth country again before I die."

After meeting and spending some time with her brother before he returned to Angola with the military, Evanjelica was happy and proud about how well he had turned out. A true hero, he had searched many years for his father, brother, and sister and he didn't stop until he found them.

Evanjelica, her son, and husband went to Chaves and started to build a house. Back in Chaves, she opened a hair salon of her own so she could work and care for her son. While the house was being built, they lived in a one-bedroom apartment with a large kitchen and tiny bathroom.

A few months passed and Evanjelica brother Gabriel called her one day asking if she could have her mother over for a visit and, of course, she said yes. Her living conditions were not too great at the time because she left a good life in the US for uncomfortable living just to please her husband. All her furniture and household items she'd shipped from America were in storage. Luckily, the kitchen was big, so she was able to put a folding bed in the middle of the room for her mother to sleep in. Even though she had money saved from working in the States, building a brick house in Portugal was not cheap. They needed to economize, so she worked long hours at her salon trying to help with expenses.

When it was time to go pick up her mother at the airport in Lisbon, Evanjelica thought this would be a challenge. She didn't know what her mother looked like, since the last time she saw her mom she was 12 years old. She was seeing her again at 30 years old after 18 years.

While waiting at the airport, Evanjelica saw these two women walking back and forth with gray hair. Then she looked at one of the lady's legs. She was wearing a dress and Evanjelica told her husband, "I remember those legs. I remember my mom's varicose veins." When she turned to face them again she felt goose bumps.

As the two ladies approached, Evanjelica asked the one who looked like her mother, "Are you Maria da Luz?"

One lady replied, "Yes, I am."

"I am your daughter, Evanjelica."

After Maria da Luz said goodbye to her traveling companion, she and her daughter hugged and cried, then left the airport, later stopping at a restaurant to eat. They spoke some more and drove back to Chaves. Back then highways didn't exist, so the drive from Lisbon to Chaves took 10 hours.

Back home Evanjelica did her regular routine. Every morning she fed her family—son, mother, and husband—breakfast then went to feed the dog and cat. Then she got ready for work.

Since her mother didn't know anybody around the area, Evanjelica took both her mother and her baby boy Rafael along with her to the salon. Her mother Maria da Luz had a chance to meet people, help Evanjelica clean between clients, socialize, and at the same time watch her grandson.

Asmodeus was not too happy having his mother-in-law living with them and would make nasty comments to his wife. "Oh, I'm working so hard so you can shove my money into your mother's ass."

Evanjelica was hurt because she had helped his family by sending them money when they were still in America. She told her husband Asmodeus, "Oh, your money? When we got married you never signed a prenup; I now wished I had made you sign a prenup. Just remember that when I married you I already had money saved and you had nothing. I am not using any of your money. I am working long hours at the salon to help provide for us. I am not giving my mom any money, just a bed for her to sleep in and food to eat. It's the least I can do; I haven't seen her for eighteen years thanks to my father. If he hadn't gone around Angola fathering children with different women, maybe me and my mom and siblings would all be together, and not broken apart for eighteen years."

On Sundays when no one worked, Evanjelica would take her mother to Spain for a visit and drive around to different cities in Portugal. Three months later Maria da Luz asked her daughter if she could take her to Setubal because she wanted to go visit her godmother. Evanjelica knew Setubal was on the other side of Portugal, far from Chaves, and she needed to take a couple of days off from work. So, she grabbed her son Rafael, her mother Maria da Luz, a change of clothing, and got on the bus to Lisbon.

From Lisbon they needed to get on the ferry to cross the Rio Doro (Golden River) to Setubal. In Setubal, her godmother Lucia welcomed and fed them, and they talked for hours. As Evanjelica was thanking Lucia for her hospitality as she was headed to return to Chaves, the godmother said:

"Perhaps your mother can stay with me for a couple of months?"

Evanjelica replied, "If she wants to it's okay with me. I feel bad for her that we are living in this small apartment, while our house is being built." So Evanjelica and her two-year-old son Rafael were the only ones returning via boat to Lisbon into Chaves.

Back home Asmodeus continued with his abusive words. "Oh, you care more about your mother than your husband. You left me for two days without any cooked food to eat."

Evanjelica replied, "I left enough cooked food in the fridge and all you had to do was warm it up, but you are spoiled and used to having me do it all for you. Maybe I should start feeding you by mouth like a baby. I have not seen my mom for eighteen years; can I enjoy her a little while she's here? You don't eat leftovers. You live close to your family; I'm sure they would feed you for a couple of days." Asmodeus had ways of making Evanjelica feel worthless and guilty that she was not a good enough wife for him. Evanjelica did everything she could to save the marriage, but was getting tired of the constant insults.

Chapter Thirteen

Bad Pregnancy, May 1992

A couple of days after she returned from her trip in May 1992, Evanjelica experienced strong headaches and severe abdominal pain; she could not even stand up. Asmodeus rushed her to ER, where the doctor asked if she was pregnant. She replied, "I'm not sure, but I'm having regular menstrual cycles, but I can't go by that. For my first pregnancy with my first-born son I bled throughout the pregnancy and I was in and out of the hospital."

The doctor wanted more information because she was a new patient, so she told him, "I am an American who recently relocated to Portugal with my husband at the beginning of January. I've done a lot of traveling between January and now." Evanjelica thought that with all this traveling, the high emotions of reuniting with her mom and brother, the hard work of opening her salon while she helped husband build the house, it had made her extremely sick. She felt weak and exhausted.

After her exam her doctor said, "You are pregnant, and the baby is dead inside. We need to induce labor." After the baby was out and the doctor had left the room, two nurses started insulting and yelling at Evanjelica that she killed her baby. She told them, "I have no need to do such a thing. I am married. I have one son and want to have more children—at least four, that's the plan."

Then her friend Odette went to visit her in the hospital and Evanjelica was crying and very emotional after losing her second baby. She was so stressed over all that she was going through and so upset for not having a supportive husband. She could not understand why she even married this man; her childhood was not good, yet once she was a working adult she had become independent and her life was great before she married Asmodeus.

Odette tried to comfort Evanjelica's anguish from the lost baby and the double insults and hurt she felt from the nurses' mean comments. She told her that those things happened all the time, and the nurses in Chaves have no respect for a woman giving birth. They don't care if the woman, or the doctor or lawyer hears; they are always yelling at the new moms asking them, "Why are you screaming? Did you scream when you made the babies? If you cannot handle the pain, why did you get pregnant?"

"Really?" said Evanjelica. "The nurses treat people that badly and nothing is done to them?"

Odette replied, "I know a lot of women have been through it. If it happened in the United States, yes, you could report the nurse and they would lose their job. But not here in Chaves."

Evanjelica was shocked concerning how they could get away with it. "Anyway," said Odette, "I came to take you home. Some clients passed by my mini market asking why the salon is closed and they need their hair and nails done before May 12 to go to Fatima (Sanctuary of Our Lady of Fátima), with the pilgrimages approaching."

Evanjelica said, "Today is May 2. I think I'll be out of the hospital sometime today."

The doctor walked in to check on Evanjelica while Odette was still there. Odette introduced herself to the doctor and told him it was urgent that Evanjelica be released later that day with all that she had to do at her salon. She also told the doctor about everything that had been going on in her friend's life, finally adding that they were horrified about the nurses' behavior.

He apologized for the nurses and said, "We are short on nurses, but I'll talk to them. Evanjelica, you need to stay here for ten days; it doesn't matter that you have clients waiting. You have a bad infection in your uterus that needs to be treated in the hospital. You are also anemic, with very low blood pressure, and you're only 85 pounds. I believe your pregnancy was bad when it originated in your uterus. That was the cause for the baby's death inside you. For all you just told me what you went through, that could have affected the pregnancy. Realistically speaking, after all the tests I ran I believe you can get pregnant again, but will not be able to carry any pregnancy to term. You would have to be on full bed rest, stress free, with a lot precautions if you want more children and I know you want them."

After the doctor left the room Evanjelica started to cry because she lost hope. Odette hugged her and told her, "It's okay, at least you already have one healthy son."

"Yes, but my son needs siblings," Evanjelica replied.

"I only have one son too, and you are still young and might be able to have more kids, but you just need to be on bed rest and follow the doctor's orders," said Odette. Asmodeus then walked in with little Rafael. When Evanjelica try to hug her son he cried and looked uncomfortable and she could smell he had a dirty diaper. Odette offered to take Rafael to her house so she could change, bathe, and feed him. Odette later found out that Rafael's bottom was raw with a bad diaper rash. Asmodeus had left his son's dirty diaper on for at least 24 hours or longer. Odette knew Asmodeus's family were not nice people and not responsible enough to care for little Rafael. So, she took Rafael to her house while Evanjelica was in the hospital. On May 11 Odette went to pick Evanjelica up from the hospital and drive her to the salon since she had clients waiting.

Odette told her about Rafael's bad diaper rash. "Oh, I see that's the reason why he cried when I held him at the hospital." She was so broken inside to know she'd married such a careless and selfish man—it was all about himself. He didn't care about anybody else, not even his own child. Evanjelica knew at that moment her marriage was going to be just as dark as her mother's, but she needed to try her best to save it. Odette dropped Evanjelica off at the salon which was right next to her mini market. She fed little Rafael and brought him right back to be with his mom. He'd missed her all the days she was at the hospital.

That day she worked on five clients and did manicures, pedicures, and styled their hair. Her body was still very weak, yet her spirit was strong. She needed to stay strong for her son and for her mother. Because they lived far from the salon she called Asmodeus to go pick her and Rafael up there. Back home, her mother-in-law told her, "I heard you worked all day after coming home from the hospital. You should not be working. Having a miscarriage is worse than natural labor. I had nine pregnancies, lost three, and had six successful ones. Every single one of those pregnancies I stayed in bed for a full month and had someone to cook for me."

Evanjelica told her mother-in-law, "Wow, that is nice your husband did that for you. I wish I had someone feeding me in bed. Thank you for your advice, I appreciate it, but unfortunately I do not have that luxury."

Her mother-in-law replied, "No, it was not my husband, he never did any housework; it was my mother and mother-in-law."

"Well," said Evanjelica, "I don't have anybody to care for me at this moment. My mom is in Setubal and the rest of my family is in the US. You don't get out of your house much and I don't expect you to walk that far to care for me so I have to care for myself and my son and husband, who never does anything around the house. He says it's not his job."

A couple months later, her mom called and wanted to go back Chaves and be with her daughter and grandson a couple more months before she returned to Angola. So, Evanjelica grabbed her son Rafael, rejecting her sister-in-law's offer to keep Rafael so she could go alone. Evanjelica went to Setubal to pick up her mom telling her she had lost a baby, that she was feeling sad emotionally, living with a careless husband without any family of her own. She was starting to fear for herself and her son's future. "Mom, I know your visiting time is almost over and you will leave soon. I have son to take care for, a business to run, and a husband that demands a lot from me, and I'm feeling very weak." Maria da Luz stayed with her daughter Evanjelica and grandson Rafael a couple months through the summer, before returning to Africa.

Asmodeus's sister and brothers were jealous of Evanjelica, a woman working having her own business, versus them only working on the farm. Evanjelica helped whenever she could in the summer on the vineyards (*vindimas*) picking grapes to make wine, cutting/mowing the hay (*malhadas*), and picking potatoes. Herself, her mom, and Rafael went to help her husband's family with the farm work, and then picked up olives for olive oil in the winter. Evanjelica always helped and she was never jealous of anyone—she wished for everybody to be happy. She was a humble, generous, and kind woman who adjusted to every situation and always treated people politely, which made her a good target for poison-minded people to bully her.

Why do people have to be jealous? Especially someone who helps them. Asmodeus's sister was always making remarks. "Oh, be careful not to ruin your nails. You are American and a salon owner."

Evanjelica would politely say, "Oh, it's okay, I don't mind and I'm happy to help." She also expected her husband to say something to his family so they would stop picking on her, but he never did because apparently she was the one who only had faults.

One summer day Evanjelica went to the salon to work, taking her son and mom with her. Then Odette started yelling at Evanjelica, "I heard you were out in the field picking potatoes with Asmodeus's family!"

Evanjelica answered, "Yes, that's correct. What's wrong with that?"

Odette continued. "You just lost a baby from all the hard work you do. You think Asmodeus's family appreciates you? I told you they are not good people. You are an American businesswoman, so make yourself important so people can respect you, because if you lower yourself by helping them they are just going to shit all over you."

"When you introduced me to Asmodeus you assured me he was good person and you would put your hands on fire for him," Evanjelica reminded Odette. "Now it's too late. I am married to him. I started a family, and I must deal with his family."

Odette told her, "No, you don't. See, I built my house here in Portugal seven years ago and I have my mini market—do you think any of my husband's family ever enters my house? No, and they never will. They are not good enough people for me to socialize with and they will never enter my house."

Evanjelica thought, *Wow, that's kind of rash, cold, and selfish.* Evanjelica told Odette, "I do not agree with treating people to be less than me just because I'm an American and have a business."

Odette knew Evanjelica was a different type of woman who would never make herself more important than anyone, as Odette knew Evanjelica never discriminated against people. Evanjelica told her friend Odette, "Don't you think you are being a little unreasonable?"

"Evanjelica," said Odette, "I will tell you this: you will never be rich, you will never be anything in life if you continue to lower yourself to lowlife people. See, yesterday a woman came to my store and introduced herself as a wife of one of Asmodeus's cousins. She asked me to tell you this. She said, 'I know you and Evanjelica are friends. Evanjelica doesn't know me; her husband Asmodeus never introduced her to his extended family, just his siblings and parents. My husband and Asmodeus are first cousins, and unfortunately there is tension between them because they think they are better than rest of the family. My husband and I are concerned for Evanjelica. On the day of her father-in-law's funeral, which by the way her late father-in-law and mother-in-law liked Evanjelica and spoke very highly of her. They would say that she's a hard-working American woman—she has a job, keeps her house clean, takes care of her son, unlike the other two daughters-in-law who did didn't work at all and only caused trouble between the family. Asmodeus's brother and sisters are very jealous of her.

"'When her father-in-law died, all the women were inside the house, including Evanjelica and her son. The men were all standing around the bonfire in the back yard talking. My husband overheard his brothers telling him that Evanjelica seems to be too smart and independent—no woman in their family ever had a business. They said in their family the men wear the pants. The brothers told Asmodeus to break that out of her, make her close her salon and if and when she asks for money to tell her he doesn't have it. They also told their brother to start messing with her brain so she will slowly start to believe that she is crazy. Asmodeus's family are known to be very manipulative and jealous people; they don't like seeing other people above them. But they don't try to better themselves either.'

"Evanjelica, it's typical in these small towns here in Portugal that people have no class, that they are jealous, they criticize, and the nicer you are to them the more they will hurt you and step all over you. They don't appreciate anything you do for them, so why bother?"

Evanjelica told Odette, "My father-in-law was a very nice man who passed by my house daily on his walks to the vineyard. I would see him through the window and invite him in. He told me he was very happy that his younger son married a nice hard-working woman—all other wives were troublemakers; his two other sons didn't talk to him or his wife for years because of their wives. And while he was alive everything was okay. I'm surprised to hear that my mother-in-law likes me because since her husband died I pass by her house daily on my way to the salon to say 'hello' to her. She says 'hello' back but with a moody face, so I thought she didn't like me. I always respected her anyway even before knowing she speaks highly of me; she is my mother-in-law. Now I will respect her even more.

"Regarding his brothers and sisters, I'm very upset I trusted them. I really thought they were my friends. I guess that was all fake and I got it all wrong." Evanjelica thanked Odette for her concern.

Odette got mad again at Evanjelica and told her, "You are too nice, Evanjelica! That's why people hurt and bully you. Do you think I ever went to help my husband's family out on their farm? No. I opened my mini market. I'm a businesswoman. I came from America, I make myself more important than them, and they respect me. You have to do the same."

Evanjelica was bothered after all Odette had told her, and questioned herself: *Is Odette telling me all of this to convince me not to socialize with Asmodeus's family? Are they really that bad? Or does she just want me to be like her and discriminate against people in lower positions?* Evanjelica could not believe she'd gotten herself in the middle of so much drama, lies, and jealousy.

It was time for Maria da Luz to go back to Angola, and Asmodeus was happy his mother-in-law was no longer in the way. Evanjelica grabbed her son Rafael and drove her mother to the Lisbon airport where they said their goodbyes. She drove back to Chaves with her son.

Two months later her older sister Carmo went to Portugal to visit Evanjelica, staying two weeks. They had lot to catch up on. One day after dinner Carmo wanted to sit on the veranda looking at the stars and asked Evanjelica to sit with her. It was beautiful looking at the stars with her older sister, even though it was a short visit. Evanjelica asked her sister, "Carmo, there is this thing that has been bothering me for many years. I know we have different fathers, but my father Ernesto was a very mean man, not just to you, but to all of us. I remember all the abuse to our mother, and there is this one thing that had traumatized me for life. I had nightmares for many years as soon as I closed my eyes. I confronted my father when I became an adult, yet he denied he ever did such a thing. I asked our brother Agostinho since he was older than me because I thought he would know more, but he doesn't remember. I asked Mom, but she didn't want talk about it."

"What is it, Evanjelica?"

Evanjelica started to cry; it was too painful to even talk about it. But she started to tell her sister. "When I was little, around six years old, I remember our mother taking all of us for a long walk, and she fought with this Black woman with small children. I later found out who she was—my stepmother. We walked back home. Later that night when my father got home he started beating on Mom so bad, he said he was going to throw her in the Rio Quanza with alligators, but he didn't. He brought her back home, tied her arms and legs with rope, put her outside the house, and ordered us not to feed her, but you fed her and gave her water to drink. I know you were also young and could have asked one of us to bring the plates back inside. All I know is that my father came home early that day, saw the empty plates and glasses near Mom.

He didn't ask any questions of who did it; he just assumed it was you being the oldest and her daughter, so he grabbed a piece of wood with nails and started beating on you. I remember you were bleeding all over. We, the youngest, were all screaming, then our neighbors came to help and call the police. My father went to jail, and Mom grabbed all of us and left the house in N'dalatando. We went to live in Dondo. That day traumatized me for life. I questioned my father several times about it, but he keeps denying it, telling me it's one of my dreams that never happened."

Carmo grabbed Evanjelica's hand and they went inside and turned on the light. Carmo, with tears in her eyes, started to take her clothes off to show her sister the nail marks all over her body. She hugged Evanjelica while crying and told her, "I can't believe you remember that event; you were just a little girl."

"I was old enough to remember," said Evanjelica. "I remember everything our father did to our mother, not just the abuse, but the cheating and lying. A lot of grownups think they can do or say anything in front of children and they will never remember . . . that's not true. Children have good memories, at least I did, and I'm sure all children are the same."

Asmodeus happened to be outside the bedroom door listening to and wondering what his wife Evanjelica and her sister Carmo could be talking about. *Were they talking about him?* When Evanjelica went upstairs to her room Asmodeus told her, "Wow, your father is a monster."

"Excuse me?" said Evanjelica.

"I heard your conversation with your sister—he is an evil monster."

Evanjelica responded, "Well, he still is my father, and I hope you don't become like him."

After two weeks her sister returned to Angola. Evanjelica dreamed of making lots of money; once her big house was built she'd have all her family over to visit often now that there was enough space for them to be comfortable.

Yet her life took a wrong turn—she did not know divorce was on the horizon, and she would be losing everything, as Asmodeus played his cards right.

Chapter Fourteen

Life in Portugal, 1993

After Evanjelica's father-in-law's death the drama and abuse towards her increased.

One of Amodeus's brother's wives told her that Asmodeus had a child with his old girlfriend, Orusula. Asmodeus never told his wife and entered into the marriage with a lie. Her married life was a living hell and she didn't know who to believe. She tried to investigate if it was true, so she politely asked her husband.

"Asmodeus, I heard you had a baby with Orusula—is that true? I know you told me you guys dated, but you never told me about a baby. It's in your past and I don't care about the woman. If there is a baby you need to take responsibility for supporting the child."

Then Asmodeus started yelling and insulting his wife. "Oh, you are crazy always inventing lies to cause problems!"

Evanjelica replied, "I'm not crazy and I'm not inventing anything. If it's a lie then I don't know why your sister-in-law would tell me something so serious." Asmodeus never liked to admit he was wrong. He did not talk to his wife for a month and wouldn't eat the food she cooked, and he slept in a different room with the door locked.

She could not understand his behavior. All she had done was ask him a simple question and all he had to do was answer, "Yes, I do have child with her" or "No, I don't have child with her." So, Evanjelica talked to the priest from their town who'd married them, and he kindly gave Evanjelica a hint that it was true, saying if Asmodeus had wanted to confess to her before the wedding he would have done so himself, since a priest cannot reveal what was said in confession. Evanjelica told the priest, "He entered a marriage with a lie and that's grounds for an annulment."

Some time passed and Asmodeus's sister Ravana, whom Evanjelica trusted and thought was a good friend, stabbed Evanjelica in the back. She was helping destroy the marriage to help Orusula get Asmodeus. After Evanjelica told her about how Asmodeus was giving her the silent treatment, she asked Ravana, "Is what I heard true? I want to hear it from my husband's mouth and not from someone else."

Ravana answered, "He's not eating your food because he's afraid you will poison him and he locks bedroom door so you won't kill him."

"Wow," said Evanjelica. "Where is he getting this from?"

"Oh, someone told him." And Evanjelica asked her who was doing this. Ravana didn't reply, but she did find out many years later that Orusula was behind all of this poisoning of Asmodeus's mind against Evanjelica because their intentions were to drive Evanjelica insane and put her in a mental hospital while she was all alone in Portugal. Asmodeus would have control of all her money, but they first needed to get Evanjelica out the way.

Evanjelica told Ravana, "It's okay. Tell your brother I'll never cook for him again. I will cook for me and my son Rafael. He is doing me a favor; wherever he has been eating now he can continue." That same day Asmodeus came home and sat at the table to eat, but Evanjelica had just cooked enough for her and Rafael. She did not say word to him, yet he started talking to her asking why she didn't cook more. She didn't answer him and ignored him for a full week.

He went crying to his sister Ravana who came back yelling at Evanjelica, "You are his wife and you are supposed to take care of him."

Evanjelica answered, "I was and I always did. Remember, I was wrongly accused of putting poison in his food. If me and my son eat the same food, how can I poison his food? How stupid is this person who told him this nonsense?"

Ravana softened her words to Evanjelica begging her to just forgive Asmodeus and be the same wife she had always been. Evanjelica asked her, "Why can't he ask for the apology himself? Why does he have to go crying to his family every time we have a disagreement? Is that why he wanted me to come to Portugal, so he'd have his family support?"

Evanjelica continued. "Your brother Asmodeus started his insults to me from the very beginning of our life together. He did the same thing in America when he went and told my family lies about me. Some believed him and some didn't. Those who believed him questioned me when I told them to back off, saying it's my marriage and it's my business now. Ravana, you listen to me. I don't know anything about your marriage, and I don't interfere in your life. I'd appreciate it if you do not interfere in mine.

"I consider you my friend and understand you're protecting your brother, but there is nothing to protect. I would never hurt him or anyone. He is a man behaving like child. I asked him one question and all he had to do was answer me 'yes' or 'no,' but instead he causes this big drama, yet he calls me crazy."

After this, Evanjelica saw her marriage go downhill. Ravana talked to her brother and he started to soften, living in the same house, not talking to his wife about what happened for two months. Evanjelica was hurt not just because he entered their marriage with a lie, but with everything else on top of it. He never apologized to his wife for calling her names or admitting he was wrong. His plan to drive her insane backfired because Evanjelica stood strong. As a result, he started hatching his next plan.

It was at the two-year mark for Asmodeus to return to the States and renew his papers. One day out of nowhere he told Evanjelica, "I know I still have six months, but I cannot go to America to renew my green card." When she asked why he responded, "I don't have my papers; my passport and green card are lost."

"How do you know that?" said Evanjelica. "They should

be in the safe box where I always keep important documents." Then Asmodeus insisted the documents weren't there, so that he wouldn't have to go back to the US.

Evanjelica was busy running her business, taking care of her son, the house, plus a troubled husband. Asmodeus was always finding ways to irritate her. She looked in the safe box and found that the papers were gone. His plan worked because Evanjelica did not see her husband's intentions.

She told him, "Then you are not going back. You wanted to come to Portugal, and you don't like America, so you don't need to go. I guess I'll have to go to the United States to renew before the two years are up so you can enter America when the time comes." This was exactly what Asmodeus wanted her to do: to get her out of their house so Orusula could be with him.

Meanwhile, Ernesto called Evanjelica asking for her help because his other daughters wouldn't help him. Evanjelica told her father, "I can only stay there a month. You have to understand my life is no longer in the US. I cannot just fly there every time you need help." She bought two plane tickets, for herself and her son, and stayed at her father's house to help him while waiting on the documents. Evanjelica wanted so badly to tell her father of Asmodeus's behavior, but she knew her father's temper, and since Asmodeus needed to enter the US, Evanjelica figured there might be conflict between her father and husband, so she kept it to herself.

After her month in the States, she returned to Portugal with Rafael who loved his visit to see his grandpa and cousins. Soon after her arrival, Asmodeus asked her to go clean the cab of his truck. She replied to him, "Why can't you do it?" He told her he needed it clean for an inspection and he was off to take a shower. Evanjelica regretted always trying to please her husband on everything—a husband who didn't respect her and who did everything possible to drive her insane.

She cleaned the truck and as soon as she opened the door, she spied the "lost" documents laying on the passenger seat. Evanjelica was furious and could not believe how stupid and blind she could have been not to see this coming. She had a chance to stay in the USA with her family and had her son Rafael with her. There was no need to go back to Portugal—there were so many black signs and red flags—yet she decided to return there to her husband where she thought she belonged, back to the destruction of her life.

Evanjelica grabbed the papers and rushed into the house. "You had the papers all along and you made me spend money on plane tickets and lose a month of work in my salon!"

With a crooked smile he had the nerve to tell Evanjelica, "I didn't put the papers in the truck, Orusula did, to get you out of your own house." Orusula was the same woman Asmodeus said had always been in his life, and he allowed her to destroy his marriage with Evanjelica.

"Asmodeus," she cried, "are all men liars or just those in my life? You called my father a monster and a liar when you found out what people said about him lying about my mother. I got mad at you for calling my father a monster because he still is my father, and I wasn't going to allow my new husband to insult him. And now you have become worse than my father, a master-in-chief of liars. How do you sleep at night?"

Evanjelica was also devastated about how much had been invested into the construction of their house—she bought all of the furniture and everything inside the house before the wedding. After two years of hard work the house was almost finished, all the interior was done, with four bedrooms, three baths, a big kitchen, a large living room combined with a dining room, a spare room for the office or salon, two big verandas back and front, with a glass-covered sun room on one side for her plants, and a two-car garage underneath the home surrounded with a vineyard and fruit trees.

With the interior of the house almost finished, Evanjelica was finally able to take her furniture and household items from storage into the house. With this interior step complete, she could cover the bricks with cement on the outside. Evanjelica was very pleased the house was in good living condition in case her family from America or Angola came for a visit. She now had enough room for them. Unfortunately, she didn't know neither her nor anybody in her family were ever going to enjoy that house. She had lost everything. She was flashing back like she was her mother Maria da Luz who never enjoyed the house she built with her father Ernesto in N'dalatando.

Asmodeus had a lot nerve to allow Orusula to sleep in the bed Evanjelica bought. She grabbed her son Rafael and drove to the salon, crying the entire way. While there, she organized herself for the day. Odette entered the salon to get her hair done, and noticed Evanjelica had been crying, so she asked her about it.

Evanjelica first said she didn't want talk about it then broke down in tears and told Odette everything. Odette felt responsible for introducing them and for deceiving Evanjelica about Asmodeus. Odette just wanted to help Asmodeus find a better life yet while doing so she destroyed her friend's life.

At this point Evanjelica didn't know what to do; she was confused, angry, sad, and her feelings were all mixed up. Should she stay with Asmodeus or leave him? As much as she wanted to save her marriage she could not allow a man to cheat on her, disrespect her, and continue to abuse her verbally and mentally while making her believe she was crazy, turning people against her with his lies and directing people's attention on her and away from him so people wouldn't see his faults. It was just problems and more problems on top of the lies and drama.

Asmodeus and Orusula had everything well planned long before Evanjelica's wedding. Asmodeus had all of Evanjelica's money under his control, so he and his family could mess with her head. She felt bad for her son and knew personally how it affected her not being able to see her mom growing up. She didn't want Rafael to grow up with just one parent. It was a big decision.

A few months passed and Asmodeus flew to America by himself, only staying two weeks. He went back to Portugal where Evanjelica was waiting for him at the airport with little Rafael. The next day Ernesto called his daughter yelling, "Asmodeus told me you didn't cook for him for a month. You are abusing him and he thinks you are cheating on him."

Evanjelica told her father, "Really? What is wrong with this man?" *Was he on drugs, under some sort of spell?* She told her father, "Do you actually believe an 85-pound woman like me can abuse your son-in-law who is a lot bigger? Everything he told you is what he himself is doing. You see, when I went to see you this summer I wanted to talk to you about my husband's behavior, but I didn't want to cause tension between the two of you because I knew he had to enter the US so his green card wouldn't expire. I was afraid if I told you there would be conflict between you two.

"When I came back home I found out Asmodeus had hidden his passport and green card to make me go to the USA and leave our house so his old girlfriend Orusula could stay with him. And I cooked every day for a full month, but he didn't eat my food. He thought I was going to poison him because I found out he has a child with Orusula. And that is the truth and what is really happening. He is the one abusing me, cheating on me, and he is twisting things around blaming me."

Evanjelica now planned to leave Asmodeus before it got worse—to go back to the United States, take her son with her, and start fresh again. Unfortunately, she didn't know at the time she was beginning her third pregnancy. As she was making all these plans to leave her husband, she started feeling very sick, having strong headaches and heavy vaginal bleeding.

She went to her doctor who told her she was pregnant, and dilating too early at the beginning of her first trimester. Her pregnancy required her to be on full bed rest with her feet elevated, taking a lot of precautions. While she was happy with the news because she wanted another child and Rafael needed a sibling, she was also nervous and afraid to lose this baby like she'd lost the second pregnancy. And now her plans of leaving her husband might not work; she needed to be careful since the doctor told her she had a bad uterus. He told her, "You already lost one baby and will lose this one too. You may even lose your life. Return to the US and do so immediately because the US has much better technology to save you and the baby. This is more serious than you think." So she took care of it right away and got plane tickets for herself and her son to return to the States in February 1995. She hoped Asmodeus would stay in Portugal so she could be free of him, but he wasn't done destroying her life.

Chapter Fifteen

Back in the USA with a New Third Pregnancy, 1995

Evanjelica was very nervous about taking the flight back to the US with her risky pregnancy—she had to put her life in God's hands. She was not aware Asmodeus had found out about her plan of leaving him and that he had bought a ticket for that same flight. She discovered this news the same day as her departure, but how did he know? Later she found out it was Odette's husband Mateus who'd told him.

Evanjelica was shocked to see him get on the bus to Lisbon. Yet she didn't care; perhaps it was best he'd be going in case something happened to her during the flight. He could watch Rafael. And once back in America, away from his controlling family, she might be able to get back on her feet. She now knew she could not trust anybody, not even Odette, who she thought was her friend. She was being betrayed too many times by too many people.

Back in the United States, she went to see her old gynecologist who sent her to the hospital to be under observation. She was dilating and had to get injections to stop the labor. She had a high fever and high blood pressure with a very strong headache. She spent a full day and night at the hospital, and the next day she was sent home with restrictions for full bed rest, no lifting, and her feet must be elevated. The bleeding continued throughout the pregnancy and she was losing a lot of weight instead of gaining it. Her doctor was concerned because the same thing happened when she was pregnant with Rafael in and out of the hospital spending two to three days there each time. At least Asmodeus could take care of Rafael while she was in the hospital.

It was a big sacrifice for Evanjelica to be on full bed rest, but she was hypervigilant, and knew she had to do whatever she could to save her baby.

After moving back from Portugal, she stayed with her older brother Agostinho for two weeks and then found an apartment from one of her old coworkers, Angelina, from the electronics factory where they worked along with Odette. As time went by Evanjelica got closer to her landlady and she realized how much better a person Angelina was than Odette. Even though Angelica was the rich owner of several houses, she was kind and sweet, always stretching out her helping hand for those in need and never looking down on anyone. She was more of an Evanjelica-type of person than Odette who was selfish, greedy, arrogant, and discriminative to people lower than her. Evanjelica came to realize Odette not only she lied to her about Asmodeus, but she was also not a good person. When they all worked together Odette seemed to be a good person because back then she worked for a boss and was not as arrogant; now she had her own business and she thought she was better than anybody else.

Evanjelica got closer and became better friends with Angelina, her sister Jacinta, and her entire family; they were all good people: sincere, honest, and loyal. They have now been friends for over 30 years. Evanjelica treasures their friendship and did realize what a difference having good friends makes to one's life and health.

Premature Birth

Heeding all precautions, Evanjelica was in and out of the hospital under complete bed rest during her pregnancy. She couldn't hold a pregnancy longer than six months; she was dilating and bleeding throughout, even with all the injections and treatment to prevent labor it was impossible. Evanjelica was anemic, had a high fever and high blood pressure, needed a blood transfusion, and had developed a bad infection on her uterus. The doctors induced labor to prevent the baby from getting affected by infection and anemia, but unfortunately he did get anemic and got the infection from her uterus. On a late May night in 1995, her baby boy, little Michael, was welcomed to this world and she met her younger son for the first time. He was 13 weeks premature and weighted only two pounds, so of course he stayed in the incubator for three months. At least he cried when he was born, while Rafael hadn't.

Asmodeus was not supportive at all. Her neighbors were more concerned about her and her children then her own husband—what a waste. Giving birth is painful, but when we hold our babies we forget the pain. But giving birth to a child and then to go home with empty hands, that pain is so much greater.

Evanjelica visited the baby daily and brought Rafael with her to see his little brother. During this time Asmodeus killed all her joy and also killed any remaining feelings she had for him. Not only did he never visit Baby Michael in the hospital, he also yelled at Evanjelica every day trying to stop her from visiting the baby, accusing her of just using the baby as an excuse so she could sleep with the doctors. After all, she didn't have to see the baby every day; she was not paying any attention to him. Evanjelica could not fight back because she was too weak physically and emotionally. Of course, she wanted to be at the hospital 24/7 with her baby, but she couldn't, and she had another child at home who also needed her. All this selfish man could think about was himself.

That's when Evanjelica realized Asmodeus didn't follow her back to America to help her or care for her and her son, but to finish breaking her as he was not done destroying her. When Evanjelica tried to regain her strength, she found a job at a hair salon while the baby was in the hospital. She needed to start making some money to get rid of this monster living with them. Evanjelica found a babysitter for Rafael—her old, retired friend who babysat him before they relocated to Portugal. She would work a full day and after work would pick up Rafael to go to the hospital and visit Baby Michael. As soon as she arrived home, Asmodeus would yell at her—it never failed. What mother would have any desire to cheat on her husband knowing her child was in the hospital fighting for his tiny life?

Asmodeus was an extremely sick man who twisted things around to make people believe he was a victim. Every day when she visited the baby in the hospital Rafael would ask, "Mom, are we bringing my little brother home so I can play with him?"

"Not yet, sweetie," Evanjelica answered. "He needs to get bigger and stronger." After three months Baby Michael was finally five pounds and starting to breathe on his own. It was time for him to come home. As soon she got the call, she left work to go pick up Rafael and they went to the hospital to pick up the baby. After being home for a full week, one night, Baby Michael turned blue and stopped breathing. Evanjelica called the 911 dispatcher who told her to do CPR on the baby. Evanjelica was afraid he was too little, but she tried anyway to save her baby.

The firefighters showed up first while she still on the phone with the dispatcher, then the police arrived, as well as the EMTs. Asmodeus, who was sleeping on the sofa, finally woke up from all the noise. The baby was transported to the hospital and Evanjelica spent the night at the hospital, sitting in a nearby chair, crying, praying; she didn't want to lose hope, and she had her doubts thinking that the baby was way too fragile. *Would he survive?* The baby was under a doctor's observation and all the tests came back negative. Everything seemed to be okay, but he was anemic and needed a blood transfusion. Evanjelica was a universal blood donor when she was single and now her and her baby needed blood. Both her boys had the same blood type as herself. So, the doctor told Evanjelica her baby needed to stay in the hospital an extra 10 days and because he was now an outpatient one parent needed to be present with him at night.

She knew Asmodeus would not do it, so she had to spend nights at the hospital with the baby, driving home in the early morning. Asmodeus left for work so she could be home with

Rafael and take a little nap while Rafael was still sleeping. Then when he woke up she would bathe and feed him and ask him to watch cartoons while she napped. She would just lay on the sofa next to him so she could rest a little.

Rafael has always been a good child, but Evanjelica was careful locking the doors. He would never go outdoors without Mom or another adult present, so she had the chance to nap a couple of hours. Then she would take Rafael to go see his baby brother. The doctor told her Michael was a trooper and fighter. "He will be okay, but we need to ensure that his lungs are stronger before he goes home." She would drive home and cook dinner for her and Rafael; they would eat together and then wait for Asmodeus to come home from work to be with Rafael. Then she would go to the hospital and spend the night sitting in a chair.

When Asmodeus got home from work she told him, "Rafael ate with me but feed him again if he wants to eat with you. I have to go back to the hospital."

At the sound of this Asmodeus shouted, "I knew you were sleeping with the doctors! That is why you caused all this commotion pretending the baby is dying. That is just an excuse so you can spend the night and sleep with doctors!"

"Is that so?" said Evanjelica. "These past three months since the baby was born I haven't gotten one good night's sleep because I can't sleep knowing my child is fighting for his tiny life. I want to be there 24/7, but I have another child at home who also needs me. You cheated on me with your old girlfriend. And you had her in my house while I was gone. During the three months the baby stayed at the hospital you never visited him. All babies have two parents, but mine only has a mom and brother. And this is not an excuse. The baby needs the doctor's care and one parent there every night. If you think I'm sleeping with the doctors we can switch, and you can sleep with the nurses so we can be even. I can sleep in my own bed instead of spending the night sitting in a chair. Our neighbors are more concerned about our baby than you." Asmodeus then shut up and didn't say another word. After 10 days the baby came home and had at-home care with nurses. Michael was slowly getting stronger, breathing on his own and outgrowing his prematurity issues. Evanjelica starting to feel more confident that the baby would be okay. She started to get more rest as well.

Chapter Sixteen

Rafael, Now Five Years Old, Starts Kindergarten, and Baby Michael Grows Stronger

Three months passed by and Baby Michael was getting stronger each day. It was now August 1995 and Evanjelica needed to go back to work. She found a private day care for the baby full time and after school care for Rafael.

At five years old Rafael started kindergarten. On his first day Evanjelica took Baby Michael in his stroller to drop off Rafael at his first day of school. Most kids had both of their parents there and some kids were holding their parents' legs crying that they didn't want to go to school. Rafael was just a quiet, sad, and timid child; he never cried and that bothered Evanjelica more than anything. She wasn't sure if he was okay being away from his mom and baby brother for the first time. So, Evanjelica gave Rafael a hug asking him, "Are you scared?"

He did not say anything, just shook his head no. She went to drop off the baby at day care and went to work. It was a long day and she could not wait for the day to be over so she could go pick up her children. Of course, Rafael needed to be picked up first at school then the baby. Rafael was so excited, telling his mom how many friends he had made at school and telling her how much he loved school. This news just made things a lot easier for Evanjelica. At least she knew he was not sad or afraid of school, so the following day the drop off was easier, as she saw Rafael running to meet his friends after giving his mom a hug. From that day on the day care provider would pick up Rafael from school along with her twin boys to watch over Baby Michael and the three older boys.

Things at home were getting tense. Asmodeus continued to go to the bar after dinner on weekdays and Sundays all day. He came home drunk causing problems. Evanjelica, who had just started to work, wanted to contribute financially. She came back from Portugal without any money and could not work during the pregnancy, and after the birth the baby needed 24/7 care. Now was the time to make money. As hard as things were getting between her and Asmodeus she was trying her best to hold down the marriage a little longer hoping Asmodeus wouldn't become physically abusive. If that happened then she would leave him. The hair salon she was working for was close to home, though not one of the best, yet between commission and tips she was bringing home a decent income. She needed to be close to home, school, and day care due to the baby's prematurity issues in case of emergency. Evanjelica knew she would change jobs for better pay eventually, and hopefully Baby Michael would keep getting stronger to make it possible for her to work a better job.

Separation 1996

Seeing Asmodeus go to the bar, come home drunk, and insult her as soon he walked in the door made Evanjelica remember stories her grandaunt told her while she lived with her those four years in Santa Cruz, Portugal. Evanjelica shared with Asmodeus this story she learned from her grandaunt. She also warned Asmodeus if he ever went to the bars frequently, there would be problems at home, and he would no longer be her husband. Yet he forgot all these promises he'd made to her at the beginning and instead chose to be a follower of the wrong influences.

This short love story is based on a true event of a couple who lived in Santa Cruz.

Back in 1975 there was this Portuguese couple, husband Antonio and wife Adelaide. They were married for a few years. They loved and respected each other and their children. Hard-working people devoted to each other and devoted to their family.

Antonio worked in construction and Adelaide stayed at home as a wife and mother. When he came home from work all sweaty Adelaide always hugged her husband saying, "You smell good, honey, now go take a shower, dinner is ready." They appreciated each other and counted their blessings.

When Antonio was done with his shower, the table was set, and she put food on the table. They said grace and ate dinner, asked about each other's day. After dinner, Antonio went to the bar to have his espresso and socialize a little with friends. Adelaide stayed home, cleared the table, washed dishes, bathed the children and put them to bed; she then sat on the sofa doing crochet, waiting for her husband to come home.

When he arrived, she would hug him and ask, "Did you enjoy your friends?" He replied, "yes." Every day they had the same routine.

One day Antonio did not feel like going to the bar—he just wanted to stay home. But his wife insisted, saying, "Honey, you work too hard all day; you should go out to socialize. So he replied, "Okay, I'll go."

That night at the bar the other guys were again talking about how they beat their wives every day, and asked him the same question they asked him every night.

"Antonio, you're always so quiet and you never told us how many times you beat your wife—every day, once week?" He replied, "Never . . . I have no reason to beat my wife. She's a good woman, a good wife, a good mother."

They all shouted at same time, "Oh, but there is always a reason to beat your wife." He replied, "She gives me no reason." They said, *"You can find a reason. Today when you go home, tell her to get a donkey and bring it inside the house; if the donkey doesn't go in, there's a reason to beat her."* He shouted back, *"What if the donkey goes in?"*

They said, *"Then tell her to make donkey go upstairs, because, of course, the donkey is not going to do that—then you have a good reason to beat her."* So as much as it was hurting him inside that after so many years of marriage he had never laid a hand on his wife, now he was being misled and pressured by this proposition of his so-called friends, corrupted influences. He was bothered, yet he had to try to fit in socially.

So, he arrived at home and told his wife to go get a donkey and bring it into the house. She asked him, *"May I know why? It's late."* Antonio shouted, *"I told you to go get a donkey."* She was shocked because after so many years of marriage he had never raised his voice until now. So, she respected his decision and got the donkey. The donkey walked into the house, happy, no problem—a special treat.

"Now make him go upstairs!" he shouted. With her hand she softly hit the donkey on its behind and upstairs he ran. So, Antonio helped his wife Adelaide bring the donkey back downstairs and into the barn. He hugged his wife, apologized and said, *"I'm sorry, this is the first and last time I will ever raise my voice to you."* Next day after dinner he went to the bar as was routine, but on his mind he knew it would be the last time; he knew these were not good friends. As he sat drinking his espresso, the other guys came around to see him, happy and hoping he'd succeeded. They were surprised after they asked, *"So, Antonio, how did it go? Did you beat your wife?"* He stayed quiet for a while, and meanwhile his friends were teasing him saying, *"It's okay, tell us. The first time is hard but it'll be easier once you start beating her every day."*

He finished his espresso, stood up, then spoke: "No, I did not beat my wife; I have no reason for it." "But we told you about the donkey!" they said. He responded, "Yes, and I did that. The donkey walked into my house and went upstairs happy and fast. My wife is such a saint, even animals obey her. So, you see, I have absolutely no reason to beat her."

He returned home earlier than usual and his wife was kind of surprised. He explained, "I am just very tired," and then told her would never go to the bar again—that he would prefer to drink espresso at home with his wife.

She agreed. She already knew husband was being tempted and pressured at the bar; she trusted him to make the right choice. She said, "Because you are in control of your life, I trust you to make the right choice.

I am proud of you for being a real gentleman, and I love you very much." Antonio told her, "And I'm proud of you for being a wonderful wife; I love and cherish you, and I love our children." I hope you love this message. We all are human beings, and we all make mistakes. We all are tempted by evil and peer pressure from miserable, poison-minded influences. We also have the free will to be in control of our lives, to be leaders on our own, and to make our own choices.

Antonio was a one-in-a-million strong spirit, a leader who made the right choice. Don't hurt your loved ones just to impress the wrong people. Being surrounded with bad influences is far more dangerous than even being around criminals.

Finally, Evanjelica saw Asmodeus as a weak-minded follower of bad influences so he could fit into society. To him, it was more important to look good to false friends instead of looking good to his family. Evanjelica's priorities were her family; they meant more to her—more than society or all the money in the world.

Evanjelica and Asmodeus were two different people, like day and night, not a good match.

One Sunday, April 1996, a warm sunny day, while eating lunch, Evanjelica asked Asmodeus, "It's a beautiful day, Baby Michael is now stronger so maybe we should all go for a ride as a family and enjoy the weather."

Asmodeus replied, "Okay, I'll go have my espresso while you get yourself and the kids ready. We'll go when I come back."

Evanjelica said, "We have an espresso machine here. I can make you an espresso."

Asmodeus replied, "Well, it's the only way I can see my friends." And off he went. Evanjelica knew he'd be home late like always. She got herself and the children ready and they waited all afternoon. Rafael kept asking, "Mommy, where's Daddy? Aren't we supposed go for a ride?"

"He should be home soon, baby," Evanjelica answered. At this moment she was furious. She hated adults playing dirty games on each other forgetting there are children in between who get affected the most.

At 6 p.m. it was getting dark, so Evanjelica started to cook dinner. Asmodeus walked in at 7, drunk. Evanjelica asked him, "Is this the way you take your family for a ride? You disappointed Rafael; he asked for you all afternoon."

So Asmodeus started up with the insults yelling, "Oh, I should do to you the same as my friends do to their wives: they beat the crap out of them."

"Watch it," said Evanjelica. "I'm not your friend's wife—I don't need you, and I never did. You can go live with your friends at the bar forever since you chose them over your family." He continued to yell at Evanjelica. She had her long hair done in a French braid and Asmodeus grabbed her braid and started to push her around.

Evanjelica told him, "Let go of my hair!"

"Oh, yeah, what are you going do about it? Call the police? I'm not afraid of the police." He started to call her bad names. She told him, "I'm not telling you again—let go of my hair!" Then Asmodeus punched Evanjelica in the face twice giving her black eye. She threw a pot of hot water at him and then hit him in the head with the pot. She called the police as he ran out. The police suggested she should go to the hospital to get checked out.

At the hospital she met with a social worker to discuss a domestic violence charge. She called her brother Agostinho to meet her at her house and he came with his wife and two sons. Asmodeus was locked inside the house afraid of the police. She called the police again and had him arrested. The police told Evanjelica he would sleep in jail and be in court tomorrow for which she should also attend. Evanjelica agreed. The judge placed a restraining order on him and gave Evanjelica full custody of the children with no visitation from the father.

At first Evanjelica didn't care and thought it was better that he stayed away from her and the children. A few weeks later little Rafael was sad all the time and he told her that he missed Daddy with tears in his eyes. "Daddy doesn't love me. He went to Portugal and isn't coming back."

Evanjelica's heart was breaking to see her child so sad; the baby was too young, but Rafael was almost six and he understood what was happening. She comforted her son by telling him, "No, honey, Daddy didn't go to Portugal. He just lives in a different house and he loves you. Mommy will call him tomorrow to tell him to come and visit, okay?" The next day Evanjelica went to court to ask for visitation, saying that her children need to see their father, especially their older son. Evanjelica was concerned Rafael might fall into a depression.

The judge first denied the visitation because the father was violent and might hurt the children, but Evanjelica pleaded her case. So the visitation was granted to Asmodeus under supervision for six months. They would meet in a public place with Evanjelica waiting nearby for a few hours. When the boys were older, they saw their father every Sunday.

Little Michael's First Birthday, May 1996

Evanjelica invited a few friends over with their children to come celebrate Michael's first birthday. Her boys had a great time with the other kids. While hosting the party Evanjelica experienced discomfort in her stomach, the pain getting stronger as time went on. After all the guests left as she was cleaning up, the pain got very severe and she was also burning hot. She had a fever and couldn't hold anything in her stomach.

She put her children in the car and drove to the ER, where the doctor told her it was an upset stomach. She said, "I've had many upset stomachs before, but never with this level of fever and pain. It is either my appendix or gallbladder?"

"How do you know that? You're not a doctor," he said.

"No, I'm not. I know my body, and I know I have an infection somewhere." He sent her home anyway. She drove home in a lot of pain and couldn't sleep all night. She was so very thirsty and still couldn't hold anything down. Her fever kept rising, but because it was the holiday weekend she called the doctor on call who told her that with her 104.4 temperature she should go to the ER again. So, she grabbed the boys and drove back to the hospital; she didn't want to bother her neighbors on a holiday weekend. At the ER they ran all the tests; they came back negative. Still at the ER, she continued experiencing a lot pain, now having been there a few hours. The boys were getting hungry and the baby needed a change.

She knew it was going to be while, so she called her landlady for a favor to come to the hospital and pick up the boys and feed them. Just as the first doctor was about to send her home, a second doctor walked up and said, "She is very pale with a high fever and high blood pressure. She normally has low blood pressure. She has been here for a few hours with no eating or drinking. I'm not sending her home just yet. I'll order an ultrasound."

While waiting for the ultrasound he did a palpation assessment on her stomach, and she would jump. Evanjelica asked this doctor, "You think it might be my appendix? I know it's not an upset stomach like the other doctor said." In a few moments the ultrasound confirmed her appendix had already erupted. Evanjelica overheard the doctor saying, "It's too late." They wheeled her into surgery and as they were doing so she asked him, "Will

I see my children again?" The doctor paused and said, "Yes, of course."

After the surgery Evanjelica wasn't waking up and the doctors had a hard time bringing her back. Finally and fortunately she woke up and the doctors told her, "You gave us all a good scare."

"Can I go home?" she asked.

"Oh, no, you need to say in the hospital for ten days for observation because your appendix erupted."

She said, "I can't. I'm a single mother with small children. They need me."

"Well, at least five days," the doctor stated. Angelina was able to watch over the boys and take them to day care. After two days Evanjelica didn't feel any pain so she asked to leave the hospital because she had obligations. She just wanted to go home to her babies, not knowing the worst was yet to come.

The next day she woke up with big blisters on her stomach like a first-degree burn. She went back to the hospital and they told her she was allergic to the surgical adhesive. As they removed the dressing, there was a big hole in her belly. She asked, "Am I open?" The doctor replied, "Yes," and after she asked why he explained that when her appendix erupted, they couldn't stitch it and that's why they wanted to keep her in the hospital longer. "How am I supposed to heal?" she asked. The doctor could not answer her. They knew they had made a mistake sending her home the first time and now things were more complicated with an open abdominal wound. She could not work at all until the wound closed.

Her neighbors told her she should file a complaint against the hospital for sending her home early; she could have died, and her boys would have been orphans. Evanjelica said, "Yes, but I didn't die. I'm here. Just because one lousy doctor makes a mistake, the entire hospital doesn't have to pay for it."

When Asmodeus found out about Evanjelica's surgery he paid her rent since he was not yet paying child support and Evanjelica thought it was nice of him to do that. *He's not all bad—he's just jealous of her*, she thought. And insecure.

A few months passed and Evanjelica saw that Asmodeus was

good with the kids. She went to court and dropped the domestic abuse charges so he could freely visit the children. The judge granted it, and told her that if at any time she saw the children in danger she should call the court and cancel the visitation. She agreed. Asmodeus started to visit the children more often and asked Evanjelica to get back together. She answered, "You have to prove to me that you can be a good father to the boys and always be there for them and treat me with respect." The children were happy to see their dad often.

One summer mid-weekday in 1996 three months after the supervised visitation, Evanjelica and Asmodeus were legally separated and not yet divorced. Evanjelica knew her ex-husband could not cook and so she felt bad for him. So, she told her older son, "Call your dad and tell him since his job is close to where we live and he lives far from his job, he can stop by our house tomorrow and I'll give him a meal to take home. And he'll also get to see you guys."

Evanjelica was just trying to make her kids happy having their father around. She would cook lunch on Sundays, and they would eat as a family, then he would take the kids for a little ride while she stayed home. She felt good seeing the kids happy with Daddy around, but she was concerned about not knowing his intentions. So, the day she asked her son to call him to pick up food, Asmodeus showed up at Evanjelica's doorstep. The kids were happy to see their dad, yet as soon as he entered her house he started to yell at Evanjelica for no reason. "Excuse me," said Evanjelica. "What's wrong with you? Just remember that we are close to a divorce where I will no longer be your wife. I am being too nice to even cook for you. I'm doing everything I can for us to be civil and have a healthy relationship for the children's sake. But I guess it will be impossible. You have not changed, and you will never change.

"Here is your food, now get out of my house. Just remember, I have sole custody of the children. I begged the courts to grant you visitation, but if you continue to insult me I'll take the judge's advice. At any time things go wrong I will cancel visitation." She handed him his food and threw him out. He stayed at the top of the stairs knocking at her door crying, "I'm sorry! Please let me in, I'll explain." She would not let him back in. He went home and called her house and told her, "Do not hang up. I have to tell you this. I know you might not believe me. I think Orusula cast a witchcraft spell on me."

"Oh, really?" said Evanjelica.

"Yes," he replied, "because I know I love you. Sunday after I saw the boys I went over to your uncle's house to help him cut wood for the fireplace and told him how you are still cooking for me. Then your uncle told me, 'I know my niece is a very independent woman; she does not need a man to raise her children, and she is a hard worker. For the children's sake go and ask her back before the divorce is final. You have to be the one asking her. Don't wait for her to ask you back—that will never happen.' Then today I got home from work and saw little Rafael's messages to pick up food you were cooking for me. I got excited and thought maybe you still loved me too. So, after work I drove to your house all excited and happy that maybe we were getting back together, but as soon as I saw you I felt this hate towards you. How do you explain that?

"All I know is I that dated Orusula nine years before I met you. I was going to marry her, but she cheated on me. When I broke up with her she told me I would never be happy with another woman. She would destroy me and any woman in my life. I know I love you and want to be with you and the boys, but we are never going to be happy."

Evanjelica told Asmodeus, "My father also used that very same excuse that he really loved my mom. He said Demonesa cast a witchcraft spell to make him hate my mother. Now you are doing the same thing! That's a nice excuse. If you choose to believe in negative stuff, instead of being a real man that accepts responsibilities and fights for the people you love, then you don't belong in my life or in my children's lives. This Orusula woman was supposed be in your past, though it appears to me that she has been in your present and probably will be in your future.

"Per all our conversations about her you seem to love her more than you ever loved me," Evanjelica continued, "and you are allowing her to destroy our marriage. Stop using her as an excuse—use yourself as an excuse if you are real man. You have to be the one making a decision."

***

Shortly after their divorce, Orusula came to the States to visit him and they married so she could stay in the US. These actions just clarified everything for Evanjelica that Asmodeus was nothing but a big, weak-minded liar, a follower of the wrong influences. One lie after the other. This man had lied his entire life so to him lying felt normal and natural. He thought he was telling the truth. Evanjelica was always a leader determined to succeed in life, but Asmodeus was just not the right partner for her. He had no determination to better himself; all he did was criticize others more successful than he by slandering their names to try to destroy their reputation. Evanjelica was much better alone than miserable. As much as Evanjelica tried to save her marriage, staying in an abusive relationship was hurting herself and her children. She knew it was going to be struggle financially. She had to save herself and her children from a bad situation.

She continued working two jobs in order to stand on her own two feet with two children to raise. It wasn't going to be easy, but she was a fighter. Even with all her physical problems and pain in her joints and her several surgeries, she never stopped. She needed to put food on the table for her children and a roof over their heads. In spite of all the emotional physical pain and marital stress she felt good. She was a mom, yet a free woman.

Evanjelica continued to allow him to visit the children freely. She felt sorry for him and wished he would change into a better person. Asmodeus realized he would not win Evanjelica's heart, and so he started intimidating Evanjelica, making her feel she would regret leaving him. He had ways of turning people against her; he had already gotten her father and stepmother out of the way. He thought they hated her, and Evanjelica had separated herself from her family since they were not supportive of her; she didn't need their negative comments. He had said he wanted to see her alone and miserable abandoned by everyone. His goal was to have her and her kids sleeping under the bridge and eating out of a garbage can. Her kids were going to be losers being raised by a crazy mother.

How could he think that she was going to go back to him, on her knees crying and begging him to come back to her, while he was going to be happily married to Orusula, the woman that he should have been married to and the one that he always loved? Evanjelica told him, "See, how can I trust you? Not too long ago you asked me back and said you hated Orusula. Now because I didn't accept your proposal, you've gone back to insulting me.

"If my kids become losers they won't be the first ones. A lot of kids out there raised by both parents become losers. I'll do everything in my power for that not to happen. I'll try to give them a good foundation, but I cannot control what they will be like when they grow up. I'll do whatever I can to support them. Even if I eat out of the garbage off the streets and sleep under bridges—is that what you wish on your children? Because wherever I'll be they will be. You are a cold-hearted man. Go be happy with your Orusula. I helped you get a better life so you can't destroy mine."

She prayed and cried and worked hard for many years after her divorce to provide for her children. She made sure they had their necessities met, and more importantly a peaceful, loving home.

She thought after the divorce she was going to be free. But just like her father did with her mother, Asmodeus was the same or worse. He tried to control Evanjelica's life even after divorce. He thought he had power over her—that she was to obey him even after they weren't married. Once remarried to Orusula, he continued to tell Evanjelica she had to ask him for permission to do anything. This went on for several years.

Chapter Seventeen

Divorce Day, April 1997

On the day of the divorce Asmodeus had an attorney while Evanjelica represented herself; she was not going to spend food money for her children on lawyers. She did not want alimony from her ex-husband; she just wanted to be free from all his abuse and insults. The judge granted her sole custody and asked her twice to reconsider her decision about alimony. She said, "Yes, Your Honor, I decided I don't want alimony from him." The judge ordered him to pay child support, which made Asmodeus upset. He started yelling that he didn't want to give his ex-wife any money.

The judge then told him, "She is being reasonable not to charge you alimony. The least you can do is pay for child support." Evanjelica asked the judge for visitation. Asmodeus refused it at first; he didn't want to be bothered with the children. The judge was concerned for her children's safety and hesitated on her request. Evanjelica added, "Your Honor, I know he was violent with me, but the children need to have a relationship with their father. They need a male figure in their lives. I don't want my children to get depressed for not having a father; it affected me growing up without a mother."

"It made you strong woman," the judge said. Evanjelica told the judge having their father around would make the boys strong and asked the judge once again for visitation. It was granted to Asmodeus one day a week, on Sunday from 11 a.m. to 6 p.m. He told the judge, "Evanjelica is just trying to get rid of her kids so she can put men in the house."

The judge looked at Evanjelica and asked her, "Are you sure you still want him to visit your children?"

Evanjelica paused and then told her ex-husband, "I don't know where you are getting this idea. I'm just getting rid of you. What makes you think I'll have another man in my life? At least not any time soon. I'm giving you a chance to have a relationship with the boys. You're lucky to have me for an ex-wife. I know some women take a lot money from their exes and don't let them see their children."

The judge then added, "She is a free woman who can date who she wants to date." He then ordered visitation, turned to Evanjelica and told her, "If you see that the boys are in danger, come to court to cancel the visitation. She said she would and told the judge she didn't think her ex would ever hurt the boys.

Out of the courtroom and back in her car, Evanjelica felt a sense of freedom. She was relieved, finally free from this ungrateful monster. Driving home was a 45-minute ride and she had her mind full of thoughts about how she would invest all her money from the house they'd built together in Portugal.

Asmodeus threatened Evanjelica to never mention the house in Portugal in court and if she did he would make her life a living hell. She was just getting out of hell; she had no attorney to represent her or defend her rights, so she agreed. Now all she could think about was how she was going to raise her children. She didn't have any money since most of her family members had turned their back on her because she went through with the divorce. They thought she was going to be knocking at their doors asking for help. She knew she was a survivor; she had faced starvation during the war in her country as a child; she didn't want her babies to go hungry, to go through what she went through, so she broke down in tears and cried while driving home.

Once at home she took a shower, changed her clothes, put on makeup and went to day care to pick up her babies who came running and hugged her legs. Evanjelica dropped to her knees to hug both of her boys. Rafael was almost seven years old and little

Michael was almost two. They filled her with joy. She kissed their foreheads and asked them about their day.

They said excitedly, "Oh, we drew pictures, see, Mommy? You like them?" When she said she loved them they also told her that they went to the park, played on the slides and swings, then had snack and sang songs.

"Wow, that is a lot. You were busy. I'm proud of you guys," said Evanjelica. The day care provider filled Evanjelica in with how smart and well behaved her boys were for such a young age. Evanjelica thanked her and left.

After she buckled the boys in the car, Evanjelica looked up at the sky and thanked the Lord for blessing her with two wonderful children. "I'm sorry, Lord, that I got a divorce. My marriage was a bad garden, but I managed somehow to collect these two beautiful flowers from my bad garden. Just smelling my two flowers every day makes me happy and gives me the strength to work, to provide for them, to move on. I don't need a husband. I don't need the betrayal of my family members. All I need, Lord, is You and for my boys to be happy. Please cover my two angels with Thy Divine Mantle. Protect them and keep them safe. Bless them to be good kids in school and everywhere to be decent human beings as they grow up, and please, Lord, bless me with the courage, strength, and the ability to work and provide for my children, to be a good mother, and more importantly, to be a good parent because anybody can have children and be a mother, but not everyone can be a good parent."

At home Evanjelica cooked, bathed her boys, and fed them. They watched TV together, then she put them in bed and read a bedtime story to little Michael. He could not fall asleep unless Mommy sang him a song. They were exhausted from all their activities and fell asleep. She kissed them good night and stood between the two single beds and crib admiring her children sleeping like angels—she would not trade this moment of peace and joy for any anything in this whole, wide world.

However, deep down in her heart she still loved her abusive ex-husband. But she had to make a choice: Should she stay in an abusive relationship and have her children witness their father insulting and yelling at their mother, calling her names—culminating in a fight that would traumatize the children, and set a bad example for when they grew up to do same to their wives? If she stayed married she would be allowing herself to get sick and upset, unable to be the healthy and happy mother her children deserved. Or she could just break free from all of it, ignore the judgment from her family and so-called friends, and choose to exist without money, but live in a peaceful happy home with her children.

She chose her children and a happy peaceful home over financial security and an unhappy relationship. Evanjelica knew it wasn't going to be easy; she would have to work extra hard to get back on her feet and provide for her children. Work didn't bother her—she was hard worker—and she felt happy and good every time she hugged and kissed her children. Her boys were her weapon—her purpose to fight against anybody or anything who would try to harm them. She had purpose to love and provide for them, to give them a good foundation and to help them grow up with strong wings so they could fly solo. She had no regrets from marrying her ex-husband; he'd given her the best gift life has to offer: her two wonderful sons. But she was happy to see him gone.

Slowly but surely, she started two jobs, one working as an esthetician in a day spa in Westport, Connecticut. Since the place was a full service spa, her boss asked her if she could also do hairstyling and pedicures. Evanjelica accepted of course. She just wanted to be busy, and with the skin care treatments, pedicures, and bridal styles, she made good tips at the spa.

Her second job was as a housekeeper one day a week. She started to make enough money to cover expenses like rent, utilities, day care, and to start a savings account. She was feeling good about herself again, and was gaining confidence, had strong self-esteem, and felt determined like she'd felt once before she married Asmodeus. The best part now was that she was a mother with a strong and good purpose to fight even harder. She was going in the right direction to meet the needs of her children, work a good job, and have loyal friends.

Chapter Eighteen

Life After Divorce, 1998

After the divorce Evanjelica continued working two jobs. She was getting a little bit of child support, not a lot, but it helped. She needed to stand tall on her own two feet. With two small children and no money it wasn't going to be easy. Evanjelica was still living in Bridgeport working at the day spa in Westport Tuesdays through Saturdays and cleaning a lawyer's house in Trumbull on Monday. On Sundays, since the boys went with Daddy for a visit, Evanjelica worked on family haircuts just doing hair—no nails or skin care. It was a good schedule—she worked during the day and stayed home at night with the boys and was making some decent income. She tried to save as much as she could. She had big expenses such as rent, utilities, car insurance, and she paid for day care by herself until Asmodeus had to pay half a few years later.

Things were going well except she had problems on Saturday when no one could watch the boys. She asked Asmodeus, but he refused her saying Sunday was enough. He would complain that he didn't know what to do with the boys and she would say, "Why can't you just watch TV with the boys or go to the park and do some activities with them? It's only one day a week. Try to enjoy them." He continued accusing her that she just wanted to be free from the boys so she could put a man in the house. Evanjelica told Asmodeus the boys were not in her way and if she wanted to put men in the house she would have already done so.

She asked her boss in Westport if she could work at the day spa Mondays through Fridays and be off Saturday, but her boss told her no since Saturday was the busiest day. She found an ad in the paper for a babysitter and hired her using her tips to cover the Saturday day care and the child care from Monday to Friday, as well as gas in her car so that the rest of her paycheck would be used for bills and savings. The boys were at home with the babysitter and her two sons. Her neighbors kept an eye out if the babysitter wasn't good. Fortunately, she was good, though after several months she moved to Florida, so Evanjelica had to start over. That was when she decided maybe she should open her own salon so that way she had flexibility of working and watching her sons.

OPENING HER OWN SALON, 1998

Evanjelica started researching how to open her own salon. She met many different people such as Brian, a salesman who sold credit card machines. Evanjelica was 36 years and still very young and naïve. A single mother, she was afraid of opening a business alone thinking it might not kick off, but she needed to work and have the means to be able to care for her children. Brian told her he'd help her find a good, safe location for her spa and for that she was grateful.

Evanjelica didn't know what his intentions were. She accepted his help and he did not invest any money in her business; he just helped with advertising to set up the spa equipment and sold a credit card machine to her. Evanjelica spent the weekend with her boys, now eight and three, painting the salon. They were happy they were going to spend more time with Mom now and they had their own playroom for toys and games. Once all was done, she had the Board of Health come inspect her business and she was approved to operate. She was relieved that finally she was able to work and have her kids with her onsite.

However, business did not become successful off right away. She lived in Bridgeport, but her business in Waterbury was a

30-minute drive away, which was the only place where she could find cheap rent and a good, busy location.

She would drop off her older son at school and the baby at day care Monday to Friday. On Saturday she'd take kids with her to the salon where they had a private playroom with their games. For three full weeks she drove daily to Waterbury and spent all day at the salon and not one client would walk through the door. She started to get discouraged. She drove back home sad and disheartened not knowing how she was going to feed her kids. As much as she tried to hide her concerns, her older son Rafael somehow knew things were not good. He has always been an old soul.

Brian would stop by the salon often and ask, "How's business?"

"Not good," said Evanjelica. "None of the advertising is working, not the TV or radio or coupons. It's not working. This is a big risk opening a business in a totally different city from the one I live in." All of her old clients from Westport were not going to make the long drive to Waterbury—Westport people were wealthy so they wouldn't bother.

Brain suggested to make some flyers that said, "Buy 3 Haircuts and Get One Free" and "Buy 3 Facials and Get One Free." So they made the flyers, and then the six of them, Evanjelica, her sons, and Brian and his sons went out one weekend to put up the flyers.

On Monday it was the same routine: drop off the kids and drive to work. To her surprise she had a few people who walked in with the flyers. They got pedicures and facials and asked if they needed to buy three or if they could just bring three friends. Evanjelica told them that they could either buy the three services or bring three friends—they just had to be sure to write down their name for credit.

That day she drove home with some money in her pocket, feeling less discouraged. She knew that once she got people into the salon things were going to be okay. She believed in herself that she provided good services and could keep clients coming back. All she needed was to get them in the door and in her chair.

Every day when she picked Rafael up from after school where he was learning Spanish two days a week, Rafael asked Evanjelica the same question every day, "Mom, did you have any clients today?"

On that day he handed her a note that said:

> *I wish my mom gets some clients and her salon gets busy so she can make money to feed me and my brother and my mom will not be sad.*

As she read the note, with tears, she dropped to her knees as she held her son tight in her arms. She told him, "Thank you, my angel. I did have a few clients today from the flyers we put out last weekend." Rafael was happy and then they went to pick up his younger brother Michael from day care.

The day care director told Evanjelica, "For a three-year-old your son is very smart and he told me you guys walked around last weekend handing out flyers for your salon." Evanjelica hugged both of her sons and she looked up to thank the Lord for blessing her with two wonderful boys. From that day on business started to improve.

When her ex-husband found out Evanjelica had opened a business he told her she had no right to open one without his permission. She told him, "We have been legally separated for almost three years and divorced almost two; you're paying me no alimony and very little child support. I asked for your help with the kids on Saturday and you refused. I have to do what I can to work and care for my kids."

He told Evanjelica right to her face, "What makes you think a crazy woman like you can run a business?" He and his wife Orusula went around telling people Evanjelica was crazy and since she'd separated herself from all those negative people they only heard Asmodeus's side of the story. He had Orusula to support his lies. In fact, she was slandering Evanjelica more so than Asmodeus himself.

As a business owner Evanjelica was going to ruin their plans. People would no longer believe them if she was indeed crazy; she was raising two children alone, operating a salon—she could not be crazy. Asmodeus and Orusula planned to intimidate her and paint her as this crazy person. They would do anything to close her down, hopefully in less than a month. But they failed. Evanjelica operated her salon for 18 years and raised her sons alone. She gave them a good foundation and they made her proud as honor students; they were hardworking and independent boys.

Time passed and business was improving. Brian stopped by the salon often and spent too much time sitting in the waiting room. Evanjelica would ask him, "Don't you have to work today?" He would reply that since he was in sales he could go anytime.

Her clients started to get uncomfortable to see this man sitting in the waiting room every day. After the clients left, Evanjelica asked him if he needed anything. "No," he said, "but since I helped you so much with setting up the salon, we get along well and my kids and your kids are good with each other, we should date each other, though I see you have men coming into the salon."

She answered, "Yes, is that problem?"

He said, "I want to make sure they are not picking you up. If we were dating I would not be comfortable dating a woman dealing with male clients."

"Great," said Evanjelica. "There is the door, please leave. Thank you for showing your true colors before any commitment. I am a career woman and I do provide services to men because I'm a unisex day spa. I'm a professional and would not allow any client to hit on me. I have boundaries and standards. I divorced my ex-husband, the father of my children, because he is insecure, possessive, and controlling. He thinks I am his property, and that he owns me. Nobody owns me.

"I appreciate all that you have done for me in helping me get set up. You will make money off of me with the credit card machine and if you need a haircut for you and your sons it will be on the house. I thank you for all your help, but I cannot accept your proposal. I do much better alone. I need to focus on my children and my business."

Brian accepted her offer of the haircuts for him and his sons every three weeks, and he would stop at the salon every day sitting in the waiting room for hours. Evanjelica had to get firm with him.

"I cannot not allow you to come here every day to make me and my customers uncomfortable." As much as she wanted to be polite, for certain people we can't be polite, or we become their target. After all Evanjelica went through seeing her father abuse her mother, and with all that she went through with Asmodeus, his family, and Orusula, she was not going to make the same mistake twice and put herself in the same situation of an abusive relationship. If a person, man or woman, shows signs of insecurity from the beginning it's just going to get worse once there is a serious commitment.

Now since business was improving, Evanjelica decided to move from Bridgeport to be closer to work since it was still a long commute. In early 1999 she rented a house in Naugatuck that had better schools for the boys than Waterbury and it was also a safer town to live in.

Chapter Nineteen

August 2000

Little Michael was now five years old and started kindergarten at the same elementary school with his older brother Rafael who was in the fourth grade. Since Evanjelica moved from Bridgeport to Naugatuck the previous year to be closer to her business, her boys were no longer in the same day care. New home, new school, new day care. Evanjelica became a member of the afterschool program at the YMCA. Their staff members would pick up the kids directly from school and keep them till 6 p.m. until the parents could pick them up. It was a good program to build strong children with lots of activities. This made Evanjelica's life a lot easier; she could work all day and then close the salon and drive the short distance from Waterbury to Naugatuck.

After four years of business in Waterbury she moved her business to Naugatuck when she saw empty retail space right across from the YMCA. It was perfect to be closer to the boys and spend more time with them with less time spent commuting. She could just walk across the street to pick them up and continue working. Most of her clientele followed her to Naugatuck, and she built up new clientele including workers and members from the YMCA. The boys were happy to be at the salon with Mom playing their games while she finished working. Gradually they started to help Mom answer the salon phone, book appointments, offer the clients beverages, and clean in between clients. Evanjelica would give them an allowance of course, even though they volunteered to help. Evanjelica knew that giving them an allowance would motivate the boys to continue helping her, and those were good working skills the boys could use in the future. They needed to learn the value of a dollar, to sweat for their money, like their mom did.

She never counted on anyone's help; she counted on her own help. If someone offered her a gift or some help she would be appreciative, but she would never ask anyone for help. She wanted to do it on her own. Things were going well. Yes, it was a lot of work, and she managed somehow to handle it.

Maria da Luz Comes to America for Christmas

Evanjelica sent for her mother Maria da Luz to come to America, and she came in December 2000 just in time for the holidays—this was going to be a special holiday. For 18 years Evanjelica prayed daily asking the Lord to bless her to find her mother; even if she could see her mom for just one day she would be happy. She knew her mother had suffered so much, having a hard life, and was advancing in age, and Evanjelica was not sure how much longer she would live. She asked the Lord, "I don't want to die without being able to see and hug my mother again. And if God can bless me with the means or possibility to make my mom's last days of her life memorable, I would be eternally grateful."

The last time Maria da Luz saw her daughter when they reconnected in Portugal was when Evanjelica was 30 years old and married with one son, Rafael. Now Luz would see her daughter at 38 years old in America, divorced with two sons, Rafael and Michael.

The holidays were special. Evanjelica wanted to spend as much time with her mom as possible to make up for those lost years. They all got together—so it was Evanjelica, her two sons, her mom, her brother Agostinho, his wife, and two sons. Maria da Luz stayed with Evanjelica, and Agostinho would take their mom on weekends occasionally. Every day Evanjelica brought her mom to the salon with her to socialize, so she wouldn't be home alone. She ignored Ernesto's threats to Evanjelica that he would kill her mother if she ever brought her to America. She told her father, "Go ahead. America is a big country. I moved away so she will be with me. I'm not anywhere near you or any of your relatives, and don't worry, even though there are rumors I'm divorced without money and am going to be knocking on people's doors, I'd ask a stranger for help before I would ask you or your family."

So, Evanjelica didn't want leave her mom home alone to protect her, in case her father decided to drive to Evanjelica's house and attack her mother. Maria da Luz would crochet and talk to the Portuguese clients. Saturdays were a special treat when the boys and Grandma would go to the salon and spend the day with Mom. After work they would go out to eat and see movies.

Maria da Luz got sick for a couple months, then her gallbladder got inflamed and she needed surgery; the following year she fell on the ice and broke her foot. It was hard on Evanjelica trying to get back on her feet by working hard, caring for her young children and elderly mom alone, plus having to put in extra care with her mom getting sick and breaking her foot. Yet it was the best three years of her life.

Evanjelica was single, free, and had her sons and mom with her. She separated herself from all of her father's relatives, her stepsisters, and everyone who was making negative remarks about her divorce or about her mom. She wanted to focus her energy on her children, her mom, and her business. The best revenge on your enemies is your success. She wanted to succeed alone without the help of a husband or family. Evanjelica would bring her mom to the boys' school events activities. Both Rafael and Michael were happy now they had not just their mom around, and Grandma too, to attend their events. In 2003, Maria da Luz had to return to Angola because her younger son Armando was sick with a terminal illness. Two years later Agostinho died from diabetes and cirrhosis of the liver, and in 2012 Maria da Luz died peacefully in her sleep. She died in peace knowing she was able to see all her children and grandchildren.

Power of Prayer

Evanjelica had her mother not only for one day but for a few months when she lived in Portugal, and then for three years in America. God answered Evanjelica's prayers and blessed her with more than she had asked for. And He blessed her mother Maria da Luz to live long enough to find her missing children, Evanjelica and Agostinho, and to meet her grandchildren.

Evanjelica prayed for protection and blessings for her boys—to be free from danger, free from bad influences, and grow up to be good, independent, intelligent young men who made their mother proud. Her boys were the beautiful flowers she'd collected from a bad garden. She wanted to give her boys rainbows and stars; she wanted to give them the world. Yet she knew she would have to work extra hard to make it happen. One thing she was sure of was that even if she couldn't give her sons a big, luxurious life, she would give them the most important thing—something she craved for and didn't have growing up: a peaceful home with lots of love and attention. She would make sure to always be there for her children. And she kept her promise to herself as a parent having her own business which gave her the flexibility to attend every school event and activity for both boys. She would overbook her appointments and work extra time on other days to be free and present the days of her boys' events. She remembered how sad she'd felt as a little girl, never having any parent present at her school events except just the one year, 1968, when she lived with her mother. Maria da Luz was present at school to see Evanjelica sing.

When Asmodeus found out Evanjelica had her mother living with her he took his ex-wife to court again to stop child support. He told the judge he was working too hard and Evanjelica was using his money to support her mother. He was also sure Evanjelica had boyfriends because he saw men going in and out of her salon. The judge told Asmodeus, "You're not paying her alimony and not very much child support. You must feed your children. She is also working and a free woman to date if she wants and she can have her mother living with her. If you are running out of money the way you claim, stop paying lawyers and stop bringing your ex-wife to court. You will not stop child support until your children are both 18 and have graduated from high school."

Asmodeus and new wife Orusula took Evanjelica to court every month to stop child support with a different attorney each time, and each time it was denied. Now being ignorant is one thing, but after so many times they were told the same thing in court. They continued to waste money on lawyers, yet *they* were the ones calling Evanjelica crazy and stupid. They made her lose days of work and that money was needed to feed her kids and mother. Then they went around telling lies about Evanjelica, twisting things around blaming her for what they were doing. They were the ones hurting Evanjelica's life and making it a living hell.

Every time the judge denied Asmodeus's petition of canceling child support, Asmodeus would come out of the courtroom and start accusing Evanjelica of sleeping with the judge. "That is why he is sticking up for you. My lawyer told me I was going to win."

Evanjelica would answer him, "Then you'd better find yourself a better lawyer. There is no winning or losing here; it's not a game—it's responsibility of feeding your children. The judge is not on your side or mine; he is watching over the children. How many times does he need to tell you to accept your responsibility as their father? Feeding your children is the least you can do since you don't care about visiting them or attending their school events." A miserable person will always be miserable and want to make everyone else's life miserable.

Orusula was the one who pressured Asmodeus to stop the child support for Evanjelica's boys and persuaded him to stop visiting them. She told Evanjelica she would give Asmodeus children herself, so he didn't have to see Evanjelica or her kids. Orusula was the kind of woman who, if things would have happened the other way around, with Asmodeus married to her first, she would have wiped him clean in the divorce. She would've taken everything from him and not let him see his kids; whatever bad intentions she had in her mind of doing to others is what she accused Evanjelica of doing. Evanjelica never stole any money from them or anybody; she proved she wasn't getting any alimony and very little child support. And she never stopped Asmodeus from visiting the boys. She had the children ready every Sunday on the day of visitation to go with their dad. Sometimes he would not show or call at the last minute with ridiculous excuses.

How could Asmodeus let his wife Orusula, who did all the talking in court, pressure him to stop visiting Evanjelica's children and have the child support stopped, now want visitation to be on her terms? If Evanjelica wanted Asmodeus to visit the children she needed to have them dropped off at Orusula's house.

The judge told Orusula that the visitation arrangement was between the biological parents and that she had no say in this matter. "Evanjelica is the sole custodian of the minors and she is giving the father the chance to visit them. He has to pick up the children where the mother tells him to do so."

How could Asmodeus and Orusula have been so cruel to pay lawyers $600 to $700 per day to stop an amount of $75 a week to feed his kids? The judge told Asmodeus, "You should be ashamed of yourself paying a lawyer $700 a day to stop food and basic necessities for your children." And they had the nerve of going around crying victim that he was a loving father while his ex-wife was the bad one who did not let him see his children. Evanjelica never stopped him.

When Evanjelica would call his house and ask him why he did not show saying that the children were disappointed and sad to be waiting for hours, Orusula would take the phone from him and start yelling at Evanjelica. "Leave my husband alone! He does not have to see those kids. You're just using your kids to steal Asmodeus from me."

Evanjelica would then answer, "Orusula, my children are with me because I'm their mother. I don't want to steal your husband; I left him and you can enjoy my leftovers; I'm giving him a chance to have a relationship with his sons."

Then Orusula would respond, "I'm going to give Asmodeus babies so he will never go see your kids ever again and I'll do anything to stop him from seeing those kids of yours."

Evanjelica would then reply, "So you bring children into this world not out of love but for your convenience, to hold onto a man and stop him from visiting his first children? That shows the kind of evil woman you are. I might be crazy, stupid, a piece of shit—whatever you want to call me—when I lived in Portugal I found out Asmodeus had a child with you, even though I knew it was grounds for annulment and that he entered our marriage with a lie, but I still encouraged him to visit your child and support him, and you came to this country illegally to marry him for security. And now you're telling me you will give him children, so he doesn't have to visit my children and doesn't have to see me? Why are you so afraid of him seeing me? If you consider yourself a better woman than me why are you going around slandering my name? Why are you so insecure? Because you cheated on him before and you fear he will do the same, because infidelity causes insecurity.

Evanjelica continued. "I did not need to marry any man for security because my life was secure and stable in this country before I married him and I didn't have to make babies for convenience to hold down a man either—that's stupidity. I had children because I wanted to be a mother. I love them more than life and I don't need a man to raise my children—I will do it alone.

"So, you see, Orusula," said Evanjelica, "you can slander my name all you want and say all kinds of lies about me; you can have Asmodeus and all the men of the world falling at your feet; and, you can have all the money and all the gold in this world, but you will always be a miserable person who is jealous and insecure. I don't need a man or money to be happy. I'm content with my life living simply.

"We reap what we plant. I have nothing, yet I am better person and happier than you will ever be."

Then Orusula told Evanjelica, "I will get rid of you so I can be happy with my husband Asmodeus."

Evanjelica answered her. "I'm not stopping you from being happy with him. I don't go to festivals in Bridgeport to look for you guys, but you and Asmodeus come to festivals here in Naugatuck and Waterbury to start problems with me. Why can't you keep him on a leash, and just stay in Bridgeport and be happy? Rest in peace, Orusula. I don't want your husband even if he dresses in gold and diamonds. He will never be good enough for me. If you don't want him to visit my children, you have no business coming around my neighborhood."

Despite all the damage Asmodeus and Orusula caused in her life many times over, Evanjelica told them she forgave them and asked to be forgiven. However, Asmodeus and Orusula would never admit they were wrong and would not accept her apology. They thought Evanjelica was the one who was bad; that's why she'd asked to be forgiven.

Asking for forgiveness is not being weak or admitting being wrong. Asking for forgiveness is about being human with common sense—with emotions and feelings—and it's about being strong. It takes a strong person to forgive and it takes even a stronger person to ask for forgiveness.

Evanjelica then realized she was not dealing with normal people; she was dealing with pure evil. All she could do was pray for them so their hearts would soften. God works in mysterious ways.

Despite all the emotional and physical pain, and marital stress, she felt good she was a mom and a free woman. Unfortunately, when she represented herself in court on the day of the divorce she did not know all of her rights. Asmodeus and Orusula kept taking Evanjelica to court every month to stop child support payments. After five years of paying for day care by herself, again Asmodeus and Orusula took Evanjelica to court to stop paying child support, but things backfired on him when the judge asked how much he was paying for day care.

Asmodeus answered, "Nothing. Evanjelica never asked me permission to put my kids in day care." The judge told him Evanjelica didn't need to ask permission because she had sole custody of the minors; she needed to work and didn't need his permission. The judge then asked Evanjelica if he was paying half of the day care fees.

She answered, "No, Your Honor, I didn't know he was supposed to pay." So, the judge ordered Evanjelica to have the day care center write a letter telling her how much Evanjelica paid for day care in full. They could only go back three years and they were scheduled back to court in two weeks.

Two weeks later she brought the invoice from the YMCA day care. The judge ordered Asmodeus to pay Evanjelica his half for a full three years, and then after that just to continue to pay his half. Asmodeus got upset and refused to pay Evanjelica any money and told the judge she would spend it on men. The judge told Asmodeus, "Evanjelica seems like a responsible woman. She needs day care and I don't care where she would use the money; it's her money. She already has paid day care in full these past three years now and you need to pay her back your half. It's over $3000 dollars."

Asmodeus started to yell that he would not pay while his lawyer kept telling him to calm down and just offer to pay, but he wouldn't. He kept refusing, so the judge ordered security to handcuff him, and that's when he said he would write a check. The judge told Evanjelica, "If it bounces come back to court so we can arrest him."

As Evanjelica walked back to her seat, Orusula got up and went right up to Evanjelica's face and in Portuguese told Evanjelica, "I'll get rid of you so you won't get any more money from us. Asmodeus doesn't have to see you ever again so I can be happy with him."

Even though she spoke in Portuguese, the judge could see the way Orusula approached Evanjelica from her tone of voice and he asked Evanjelica, "Did she just threaten you?" Evanjelica could not speak a word and could not believe how stupid a woman Orusula could be to make such a threat right there in court. What made her think she could get away with such behavior just because she controlled weak Asmodeus? Did she think she could control the judge and the law?

Evanjelica was speechless. The courtroom was full of Spanish American people who told the judge about the threat Orusula made to Evanjelica. Orusula got arrested with a restraining order that she no longer could be in court or anywhere near Evanjelica. Since she couldn't go with Asmodeus to pick up the children, Orusula stopped Asmodeus from visiting his sons, so he didn't have to see Evanjelica alone when Orusula was not with him.

Chapter Twenty

Words of Encouragement

Evanjelica continued working long hours, but she was happy. The boys were doing well in school, her business was thriving, and she was meeting more people and making friends.

While raising her children, she encouraged them to be good citizens and leaders. She expected nothing less than straight A's. Evanjelica knew that the boys may need a more detailed list of what she meant, so here it is for you:

To be successful, you need a good education, determination, and you need to know the value of hard work. You also need to be a real gentleman to women, be a decent human being to everyone, and treat everyone with respect.

Do good deeds, because if you plant a good seed, you will collect good fruit.

Be careful about not fathering any children without marriage; you need to be financially secure, responsible, and settled down before bringing any children into this world. Because anybody can have babies, but not everyone can be a parent. And it is important to be a good parent because children don't ask to come into this world. Whoever brings them should be responsible and be there for them to raise them until they grow wings to fly solo.

Rafael and Michael were both smart and had good grades in school, and as they grew older and reached their teenage years, they would tell their mother, "Mom, you have high expectations.

Our friends take home B's and C's and their parents don't say anything."

Evanjelica would reply, "You don't know that. It's whatever your friends tell you—what really happens in their home might be different. Besides, I'm not your friends' parent; I'm your parent. And, yes, I have high expectations for my boys. You see, as a little girl I was ambitious and wanted to get as much education as possible—to grow up and have a high position in life. My dreams were destroyed, and my life took many wrong turns. The civil war in my country forced me to move to two other countries. I grew up with a negative, old-fashioned Portuguese father who didn't believe women should be educated because no man would ever marry an educated woman. I also had an abusive stepmother who wanted me as her slave to do house chores alone. She didn't want me to go to school at all.

"Luckily, I was able to finish high school living with my grandaunt in Portugal before I came to the States. And as I grew older, I put myself through trade school and got a degree. At least I have a career and it came with a lot of sacrifice—though not a lot education like I wished for, yet it's something.

"I want something better for my boys. You guys were born and live in America, the country of opportunity, and you live with your mother, a positive parent who wants the best and most brilliant future for her children. You both are doing well in school and I am proud of you both, and I want to be even more proud of you. Never allow anybody to talk you out of your education, like my father did with me; also, your father, my ex-husband, after I married him wanted me to give up hairdressing to go clean houses because I gave men haircuts and he didn't like that. I told your father I had no problem cleaning houses. I did housekeeping before and could do it again, but that's not what I went to school for. I will give up hairdressing when my legs and arms give up on me. It's good to be multi-skilled, but your career and your education follows you everywhere. Nobody can take that away from you.

"Please, my sons, I believe in you guys. I have faith in both of you. Believe in yourselves, have faith in yourselves, follow your dreams, climb high, and do not stop until you reach the stars. You will encounter challenges on your path of life—that's part of growing up. Face those challenges with your heads held up high, and your hearts wide open.

"Pursue your dreams, do not stop until you are successful.

"Do not do it for me; do it for yourselves. Just remember, the choices you will make in the future will be your own choices. If it's a good choice life will reward you and will make me proud and happy. If it's a wrong choice life will teach you consequences and that will make me sad and disappointed.

"Never compare your life with anyone, so be yourselves, make yourselves proud, and make your mother proud. Be strong, be brave, be wise, and be courageous to overcome any obstacles. Life might keep us apart, with the distance of many miles between us. My heart will always be with both of my sons and my future grandchildren every step of the way. I love you guys so much; I want the best for you. Use your young smart brains for good and you will have a brilliant future."

* * *

Rafael was her most affected child when his parents separated when he was five years old. Now much older he told his mom, "You work a lot of hours and take time out of work for us. Why can't Daddy do the same?" Evanjelica did not know how to answer her son. She told him that Daddy may or may not show up, but Mom will always be there. And she did attend every single event, field trip, and she volunteered in the school library one day a week for a couple of hours. To Evanjelica giving her boys her attention and quality time was much more important than spoiling them with expensive games or clothing and not being there for them. She wished that instead of having all his properties and money, her father would have given her and her siblings more of his time and attention.

Evanjelica was not rich—she raised her children simply—she wanted to make sure she was present at all times to witness their achievements. She would always take the boys out for special treats to encourage and reward them every time they made her proud, like being on the honor roll or bringing home award certificates which she posted on the walls of their rooms. Evanjelica felt blessed and thanked the Lord daily.

Asmodeus never cared to visit the boys when they were younger. They needed their father, yet he wanted nothing to do with them. He was always insulting Evanjelica, taking her to court every month. Evanjelica believed that every marriage that ends in divorce is both parties' faults. It's two people getting married and it's two people getting a divorce. Some couples tend to have one party blame the other and say it's all their fault. However, in Evanjelica's case she had some faults, but she also tried her best to save the marriage. She didn't believe in divorce, but Asmodeus married her with ill intentions. He was selfish and a player who liked to play with people's minds.

Evanjelica wanted her children to be raised by both parents. She missed not growing up with her mom and she wanted better for her children, and Asmodeus made it impossible for her to save their marriage by making her believe she was crazy. She did seek psychiatric help when she realized she had two small children to raise and wanted to possess good mental health for them. After evaluating her history, the counselor told her, "Crazy people don't look for help and they never admit they have issues. You took a very strong and brave step to ask me for help. You are capable of raising your children. I see you dress nice; I see your children are clean; you are a hairdresser and your clients keep coming back. Dealing with the public is a difficult job and if you can please your customers, then you are not crazy like your ex says you are. He's doing this to control you because he's jealous of you. You are a threat to him, and his insecurity makes him want to lower you to make himself feel better than you."

The counselor told Evanjelica to continue to do what she was doing. "You are a strong woman and a good mother. Don't let any man or anybody else ever put you down again. Use your kids as your weapon. You need to stay strong for them like the step you took today. Now I need you to bring your ex-husband in to see me." Evanjelica told the counselor that that would never happen—he would not come.

The humiliation she went through after the divorce was far worse than seeing the counselor. Whatever Asmodeus and Orusula said about her was affecting her life financially and emotionally. People who believed their lies spit in her face and she suffered rejection to the point when she thought life wasn't worth living that way, but she kept the words of the counselor in the back of her mind: "Fight, you need to stay strong for your children." Sometimes we have to let go of our pride and subject ourselves to humiliation for the people we love, even if we think we are not at fault. Evanjelica did so for her children and she stayed strong for her children, so it was worth the humiliation.

Asmodeus and Orusula did everything to hurt Evanjelica, but they were also hurting innocent children. They would show up at the same summer festivals Evanjelica attended with her sons. Asmodeus would stare at his ex-wife nonstop, which made Orusula even more mad when she asked him to dance and he would refuse; he'd just stand there looking at Evanjelica. So, for revenge Orusula would slander Evanjelica's name, twisting things around and telling lies, making her out to be a bad person. A lot of people started to believe them because it was two of them against one saying the same thing. They never heard Evanjelica's side of story because she'd moved away to raise her kids in peace, away from toxic, negative people. She knew it takes a strong person to forgive and an even a stronger person who always asks for forgiveness.

RAFAEL AND MICHAEL'S TEEN YEARS

Rafael had been such good young man that the YMCA, where he and younger brother Michael attended after school and summer camp, hired him as soon he turned 16 as a role model to supervise the younger kids at the parks, as well as a lifeguard at the pool.

He was happy to earn a full paycheck and not just an allowance from Mom. Since he was a child Rafael had been very mechanically inclined and he attended a technical school to improve his skills. At age 17 his school found him an internship with an aircraft manufacturer as an electronics technician making $19/hour, more than his mother. He worked for them during the summer and then he finished high school. At the end of his two-month internship, he told Evanjelica that the company was hiring, so Evanjelica applied to work at that company.

In November 2008 Evanjelica was hired as a QC inspector of aircraft manufacturing on second shift, with a starting pay of $23/hour with excellent benefits. She would work at her salon four hours in the morning during the week and a full day on Saturdays. She was home on Sundays with the boys since their father had stopped visiting them.

The boys were now older with Michael being 12 and Rafael earning his driver's license at age 17. Evanjelica taught him how to drive both stick shift and automatic. When he turned 18, Rafael wanted a used Pontiac Firebird. Evanjelica asked him, "Why not get a newer, safer car?" He told her that was the one he wanted so he could take it apart and remodel it. It was a five-speed and Rafael changed the transmission into six speeds. That car had been his hobby for many years. Once he finished high school he got himself rehired full time at the aircraft company for the day shift at $25/hour. He made enough money to buy himself another vehicle to drive daily to work while he took his time working on his classic car.

Both boys were old enough to stay home eight hours while she worked. She would leave them dinner and be home at midnight. That job at the aircraft manufacturer helped Evanjelica become financially secure since it offered good pay and excellent benefits. She could buy a new home for her and her children instead of renting, and she could also buy a car for each son.

Unfortunately, after eight years of working for that company she lost her job, but by then the boys were adults and out of house and both serving in the military. Both were married so she just worked at her salon full time again.

In the summer of 2009 Evanjelica planned a party for both of her boys' graduations—her older son, Rafael, graduated from high school and her younger son, Michael, graduated from the eighth grade. Evanjelica invited Asmodeus and his family; she knew he did not care for her kids and might not show up. Orusula was always looking for an opportunity to slander Evanjelica's reputation and she thought this would be a good chance to turn Evanjelica's friends against her since Asmodeus and Orusula had already turned so many other people against her. They had failed previously to break her, yet now maybe they could turn her closest friends and clients against her.

Asmodeus, Orusula, and their two kids showed up at her party. Of course, they started insulting Evanjelica just by sitting in one corner not eating any of her food. Their kids asked for cake, but both Orusula and Asmodeus reprimanded the kids telling them, "No, we don't trust her food." The other guests overheard that and thought it was weird, but they continued to eat and enjoy the party. Evanjelica did not cook—the party took place in a small hall where she had all the food catered, including the cake. Orusula's kids still insisted they wanted cake, so Evanjelica told her boys, "Take some cake to your little siblings." Evanjelica stayed away from them and continued talking to her guests. Orusula got up fast and went to the table serving cake where her children were standing like she didn't trust anybody. Her boy and girl ate the cake, then they started running around playing with the other small children.

Soon, her son vomited, and Orusula shouted that the graduation cake had poison in it. "Evanjelica is trying to poison us!" Then one of the guests shouted, "Well, then we are all poisoned. We all ate the cake—how come your girl didn't vomit if the cake is poisoned? Both kids ate it and both should have been sick."

Then Evanjelica told them, "Is that why you just sit in the corner and don't want to eat? I didn't make any of the food or cakes. I did not serve your kids—you did that yourself. Don't accuse others of your dirty intentions. I have a heart." Her sons had their girlfriends at this party, Emily and Claudius (who later became the boys' wives). They were all socializing at one table as young teenagers and did not noticed the incident until Asmodeus and Orusula approached them saying goodbye. "Why so soon?" the boys asked.

Orusula said, "Your mother just insulted us." Asmodeus and

his family left. Rafael and Michael approached the table where Evanjelica was sitting asking their mother what had just happened referring to what Orusula had just told them.

Evanjelica replied, "They didn't eat our food and they thought I poisoned their kids, both of whom asked for cake. Your father and wife shouted, 'No, we don't trust her food!' When I told you guys to go serve them, Orusula herself went to the table to serve them. Her boy vomited. It's normal; he was running around, but Orusula shouted that it was the cake that had poisoned him. The girl didn't vomit and none of the guests did. If I had poisoned the cake it would have killed everyone here, not just her child. I did not serve her kid—she did. She insulted me. All I said after her accusations was, 'Don't accuse others of your bad intentions and I have a heart.' How is that insulting her?"

Both Rafael and Michael told their mother, "You see, Mom? We told you not to invite them." One of the guests told Evanjelica people like that cannot be trusted and maybe she poisoned her own kid and if so, then all the food needed to be thrown out. Evanjelica's mind didn't go there because she didn't think badly of people until she was hurt. She did not throw out the food, as it had cost her a lot of money and she didn't like to waste anything, but she was still bothered all night by this incident.

It didn't take long for Evanjelica to hear the rumors about how she'd tried to poison Orusula's kids. Evanjelica had suffered a great deal since Orusula entered Asmodeus's life because Orusula made it her number one hobby to poison Evanjelica's reputation.

A few weeks after the boys' graduation party, Asmodeus took Evanjelica to court with another lawyer this time to see if he could avoid paying child support for Michael, since Rafael had already graduated from high school. This time Orusula was not with him due to the threats she'd made to Evanjelica and she was afraid of being arrested again in court. Every time he took Evanjelica to court something backfired at him—either he had to pay insurance on his children or pay half of day care, and, ironically, Evanjelica would not have known these things if Asmodeus hadn't take her to court. The judge always hit him back with something. So now he took Evanjelica to court again because one boy had graduated, and he needed to stop the child support. The judge told Asmodeus, "Now instead of $75/week, you will pay $125/week for your younger son for next four years until he graduates from high school." Asmodeus didn't have his wife to talk for him, so he started crying like a baby accusing Evanjelica of trying to poison Orusula's kids at the party.

"Your Honor," Evanjelica told the judge, "I didn't make any of the food or cakes; I had the party catered. Asmodeus and Orusula did not eat anything there, but their kids wanted cake, so his wife went to serve them herself. The kids were running around . . ." Evanjelica told the rest of the story telling him that he and his family tried to poison her in Portugal; that they liked to accuse other people of their own dirty intentions. Evanjelica also told the judge Asmodeus had hurt her boys many times by not showing up on visitation day when her children had waited for him for hours.

Asmodeus started crying, telling Evanjelica, "Oh, do you know how hard it is for me to work long hours at work and come home and cook and clean and take care of the kids?"

Evanjelica answered him, "Oh really? No, I don't know. Perhaps you forgot I'm a single mom and I do all of that and so much more. I have to be a father and mother, a provider to my boys, which by the way, they are also your children. You never wanted any responsibility for them and always told me that they were my kids. I didn't make them alone—you did most of the work. What happened to your wife? Why can't she do housework? You never did anything around the house when we were married."

After they got out of the courtroom, Asmodeus told Evanjelica, "My lawyer told me I was going to win. The only reason you won is because you're sleeping with the judge." His lawyer looked at Evanjelica, shook his head and said, "I never said such a thing. I spoke with both your ex-husband and his wife, who is demanding and loud—she did all the talking. I explained to both of them they cannot stop child support until the youngest boy is eighteen or has graduated from high school, but they insisted they were going to pay me a lot of money. I had to convince the judge, so I told them I'll see what I can do—maybe reduce and not cancel the child support, but instead it got increased. I'm sorry it didn't work in his favor. Good luck to you, ma'am." The lawyer walked away and Evanjelica unlocked her car.

Asmodeus shouted, "I know you're sleeping with the judge—is he better than me? You know I love you, but Orusula has power over me." Evanjelica turned around, furious.

"You're nothing but a coward and a cry baby! You have been telling me since right after the wedding that you love me and can't love another woman the way you love me, but Orusula won't allow us to be happy. First you enter our marriage with a lie by fathering a child with another woman. And then right after the wedding you start off with the wrong attitude that we aren't going to be happy. How many times did I tell you that it was the wrong attitude to enter into married life? You never stopped being rude and small-minded with me.

"Orusula destroyed our marriage because you are weak and afraid of her and you allowed her to do so by giving her power. Why can't you grow up and be a man? Stand up to her and say no? You always said no to me when I asked you not to go to bars and follow bad influences. You still went, didn't take my advice, and that's the same as saying no. Orusula told you not to come visit my kids. You do exactly what she tells you. Are you that afraid of her? Or are you just a player? Now you're married to her and you're using me to make her jealous. No wonder she attacks me everywhere she sees me. If she is that powerful, why can't she change the judge's mind and force him to stop the child support, so you don't have to bring me to court every month and make me lose time at work?

"You know how many times you hurt my boys? A few times I asked you to just attend their school events; it would have made them so happy to see you there. I'm raising my boys very simply without a lot money, but I'm giving them the most important thing: my attention, my time, my presence, and my love. All of that meant a lot more to me growing up. I didn't have these things and I want to give my children what I didn't have even if

I struggle financially. Money will be spent and disappear, but my presence and love will stay with them forever. I'd appreciate if the two of you would leave me the hell alone. I've moved on." She got in her car and drove off.

Chapter Twenty-One

Military Service, September 2013

When Michael turned 17 years old Evanjelica bought a Jeep for him because he wanted a bigger vehicle, so the Jeep was perfect. Like his older brother, he also attended a technical high school and enlisted in the US Army at school without Evanjelica's knowledge, but since he was under 18, she needed to sign to support his decision. Rafael worked for the aircraft company, and after two years, decided to join the US Navy. Evanjelica was not happy with both of her sons' decisions, as she feared for their safety—her heart was crushed inside. Both boys were honor students with grants for college—there was no need for them to join the military, yet that is what they wanted, and she was supportive of their decision, and prayed for their safety.

Since they were both leaving the same year a month apart, Evanjelica coordinated a "Sendoff to Boot Camp" party for her boys, inviting her friends and many of her clients who saw the boys grow up. Both boys' classmates and Rafael's coworkers and friends, plus his fiancée Emily and her family were invited. There were over 100 people at the club. As she was writing invitations and preparing for the event, tears rolled down her face. She was preoccupied with concern about her sons' safety, hoping they would not be deployed where there was war because she had been through a war. Not only had she faced starvation, but she had experienced the trauma of bombing, and possible injury and death.

Evanjelica just had to put it all in God's hands and pray for her boys' safety as well as all the men and women serving in the armed forces.

Rafael was now almost 22 years old, and time was flying by before his departure. He decided to marry the love of his life, little Emily, the girl he had been dating for five years.

Evanjelica loved sweet and cute Emily as her own daughter. She got to know her well because Emily was over at the house often and they went on vacations together.

The wedding would be a small, simple ceremony; the young couple only wanted immediate family and friends present—just twenty guests. It broke Evanjelica's heart because she envisioned her boys would each have a big, beautiful wedding and she wanted to give Emily a bridal shower, yet there was not enough time since the young couple had given Evanjelica such short notice. She hoped Rafael and Emily would want a bigger ceremony and church wedding in the near future, but sadly that did not come to pass after 12 years of being together and seven years of marriage.

The wedding took place in April 2013 and the sendoff party fell on the beginning of June 2013. Rafael left right after party a few days later, before he turned 22. He spent his 22nd birthday at bootcamp.

Michael left after July 4, 2013. He had to first graduate from high school which happened in late June. At the sendoff party, Evanjelica tried to hold off tears since she didn't want her sons to worry about her. She knew they both carried a big load on their shoulders to go serve their country. They needed to focus on their journey, and not have to think of Mom being sad because they left. She tried to smile throughout the entire event and had put together a nice speech of encouragement and support, wishing her boys good luck and a safe journey. She wanted them to know even though she was going to be alone and emotional—both of her sons were leaving at same time to serve their country—she was going to be strong and she was going to be okay. After everybody ate and danced a little Evanjelica announced for the guests to help themselves to more desserts as she was now ready to share her speech.

She started by thanking everyone for their presence. Most of them have been in the boys' entire lives and had seen them grow up, and now were seeing them leave to serve their country. She thanked all who had stretched their helping hand to her boys in times of need and helped out with the babysitting.

Then Evanjelica started reading her note to her sons:

> My sons, you both have made me very proud. As a woman raising two sons alone it was not easy—boys need a strong voice, a male figure—and I was always concerned for your safety and how you would turn out. As a mother, my wishes and prayers are for both of you to do well in school, have good grades, and grow to be decent human beings, respect others, and be determined and successful. You both fulfilled my wishes; you are honor students with grants for college, but you both decided to join the military and serve your country instead.
>
> You are both bright young men with many good skills and a brilliant future ahead.
>
> God has answered my prayers; you are both a gift from above, and I could not have asked for better sons. I know I was not a perfect mother. I made mistakes, but I did try my best to be a good parent, and provide you with food on the table and a roof over your heads. And more importantly, a loving peaceful home.
>
> I have given you both a foundation, and showed you the keys to success: hard work, determination, and willpower.
>
> Today you both showed me bravery and courage.
>
> It's your turn now to go forward and build a happy successful future for yourselves with the strength of two things I work so hard to give you: roots and wings. Today I am a proud mother of a sailor and a soldier.
>
> We will soon be apart, separated by many miles. Bon voyage, my sons. Be safe, be strong, be courageous—my heart will be with both of you every step

*of the way. I love you, my sons. May God Bless and
protect you both every day.*

*I give my sons to you:
I held them as infants:
kissed them as boys.
And throughout the years they became
my greatest pride and joy.*

*I love them more than I can say,
their lives more precious than my own.
Gone are the whims and notions,
of the little boys that I have known.*

*For the years have passed so quickly,
since time it all began,
and now they stand before me
with the convictions of a man.*

*They want to serve their country,
they state it aloud and with pride.
As I try to sort out the emotions
that I am feeling deep inside.*

*A union of uncertainty and fear,
which I cannot control,
and the allegiance that lies deep within
my patriotic soul.*

*I trust that my years of guidance
will serve as a foundation
as they perform their duties requested
by their beloved nation.*

*God, please guide them as they travel
to the places our sailors and soldiers have bled,
and walk with them to pathways
where those heroes' feet have tread.*

> *Oh, sweet Land of Liberty,*
> *humbly I give you my sons,*
> *praying you will return them safely home,*
> *when their work with you is done.*

Many of her guests were concerned for the boys and for Evanjelica, thinking it was too much for a mother to handle, especially being all alone with no husband to support her and comfort her as her sons departed to explore the world. She must handle it all alone. She did have her boyfriend Paul and he was supportive, but he lived an hour and half away and they only got together on the weekends.

After the party when the guests had left, Evanjelica stopped smiling and did more crying and praying. She prayed daily that the Lord would bring all of them back home safely to their families. Evanjelica's house felt so big, empty, and lonely. She checked their rooms every night as she got home from work. The beds were still made—no mess, the rooms weren't noisy, and even the 13-year-old cat they'd rescued when she was two weeks old was lonely not to have the boys there to play with her. No TV, no games, no radios—all is quiet now.

Evanjelica got the first letter from her son Rafael at boot camp. It was a letter using real pen and paper, not text or typed up on a computer; she knew this was good for the boys. Evanjelica immediately replied to her son's letter and checked the mailbox daily. Michael left two weeks after his brother so it would take a while to hear from him, but she did get a letter from Michael the following week, and then every week she would get one letter from each of her sons. She saved all their letters in a safe box along with their military pictures and boot camp graduation videos.

In August, Evanjelica flew to Great Lakes, Illinois, for Rafael's boot camp graduation, and in September she flew to Fort Jackson, South Carolina for Michael's ceremony. It was emotional, overwhelming, and heartbreaking seeing all those baby faces of young men and young women serving their country.

After graduation, one son went to Pensacola, Florida, for a month and he was later stationed in Lemoore, California, then nine months aboard an aircraft carrier. The other son went to Monterey, California, for a couple of months, then to Texas and then he was deployed to Germany.

Evanjelica continued her normal life after eight years, returning to full-time work at the salon after she lost her job at the factory. She still had to take care of the house, rake leaves in the fall, mow the lawn in the summer, shovel snow in the winter—all by herself now; it was much more fun when the boys were around. They worked together and then had a snowball fight.

For Christmas 2013 both boys had leave to come home and spend the holidays with Mom. Evanjelica was excited, decorating the house more beautifully than in previous years. She cooked and baked and Michael brought home some of his soldier friends and asked her if it was okay to invite his old girlfriend that he had broken up with before leaving for the army. Since Rafael had his wife there Evanjelica said yes. She just wanted to see her boys happy.

This was the last Christmas they would spend together as a family because the following year Rafael was deployed to an aircraft carrier from August 2014 to June 2015, so only Michael flew from Germany to Connecticut to spend Christmas with his mother and propose to his girlfriend. Evanjelica thought Rafael was too young to be married at 22, and Michael was even younger—getting married at 19. But if they are serving their country young, they can get married young. In February 2015 Evanjelica planned a bridal shower for Michael's bride and her future daughter-in-law Claudius.

Evanjelica's boyfriend Paul was a nice man, widowed, and a single father of a boy and girl. They met in 2013 before her sons left for the military. He was supportive of Evanjelica and her sons. Every Saturday he would drive from Massachusetts to Connecticut to meet Evanjelica and keep her company since she was now alone. They did fun activities and Paul was also a handy man who helped Evanjelica a lot around the house.

Rafael had a homecoming from deployment three days before his brother's wedding. When he arrived in San Diego Emily was there waiting for him. They drove to Lemoore, California, where they were stationed and then flew to Connecticut the next day. It was kind of a tight schedule since he was the best man, but Michael was prepared with a backup in case his brother didn't make it back in time. It all worked out, though. Evanjelica was the chauffer picking up everybody from the airport the day before the wedding.

Rafael finished the five years of his military contract with an honorable discharge and was working long hours and going to school for his master's degree in engineering. He left the Navy base the same day Michael's daughter Cristina was born. Now Rafael and his wife Emily were on their own and had to find a place to live out in the civilian world.

Evanjelica offered them her house while they were still on the East Coast; they could stay there until they got situated with jobs and eventually could find their own home. They refused to go back to the East Coast since Rafael had to continue college in California. The young couple, with no household experience, in the largest and most expensive state in the United States and just recently finished with the military, had a hard time finding a place to live. Nobody would rent to a young couple with no rental history. Finally, Rafael's former employer gave him a letter of recommendation to an apartment building's management so they could have a place to live. Rafael and his wife Emily both worked to meet expenses. They had to stay in California to finish his studies then relocate to a cheaper state.

Michael finished the five years of his military contract also with an honorable discharge and he relocated back to America. H was the only one working to provide for his family since Claudius was a stay-at-home wife going to school, and little Cristina went to preschool.

Evanjelica continued her strong relationship with both of her sons and their wives. She speaks to her grandbaby mostly by phone since everyone is in a different state. They all got married young and with military life there is a lot of moving. They will grow up hopefully into mature and responsible young adults.

Rafael and Michael made their mother Evanjelica proud. She

sees her boys being brave, strong, intelligent, and independent leaders.

Evanjelica raised her boys to be decent human beings—to learn how to say thank you and respect people who helped them and how to apologize and say sorry to those whom they hurt. She also encouraged her boys to have a relationship with their father if he ever asks them to talk.

What Evanjelica never expected was that Asmodeus and Orusula would try to lie to the boys and turn them against their mother, while trying to get credit for the boys' successes even though the they knew the truth and saw everything their father and stepmother did. The boys do not believe any of the lies.

If they'd become failures Asmodeus would not want anything to do with them; he would actually rejoice and say, "I was right; the boys became losers because they were raised by a crazy mother." Both Rafael and Michael are good, responsible, and independent young men and their father will never give credit where credit is rightfully due; instead, he will say that it was their mother's fault he didn't visit them.

Since both sons were planning not to return to the East Coast, Evanjelica already had her house on the market and decided to relocate to the West Coast with its warmer weather. She had to sell most of her furniture and household items and just ship the necessary items, then drive cross country. One new and big adventure.

To my boys: *I always be there advising you, encouraging you, to change your life, and overcome all obstacles. Life may keep us apart in distance with many miles between us, but my heart will always be with both of you, my granddaughter, and future grandchildren every step of the way.*

KARMA AND THE POWER OF FORGIVENESS

Ernesto had abandoned his sons Gabriel and Armando in Angola and told his family that Maria da Luz was deceased, and that he never left any children behind. He ignored his older son Agostinho living in US to please Demonesa and he gave up on Evanjelica because she was divorced with no money and two children to raise when she most needed him. Armando died at age 30 in Angola from a terminal disease and Agostinho died at age 48.

Her father only cared about Demonesa's kids. He found himself disabled in a wheelchair alone in Portugal and abandoned by all the rich people he'd thought liked him, but they only did when he had money and life was good. Now he decided to turn to his son Gabriel in Angola who was a sergeant in the air force and who Ernesto had abandoned when he had asked for help, telling him to have Evanjelica call him and saying that he needed to talk to her after all these years. Years and years earlier Evanjelica tried to talk to her father, yet he refused her, as she wasn't good enough; she was poor and she'd left everything in Portugal. He'd thought she was just after his money, but now he wanted to talk to her. So, Evanjelica called her father at Gabriel's request and Ernesto asked her, "Since your children are now adults and married, you are alone and free, can you come back to Portugal to live with me? I really need your help and company."

Evanjelica asked him, "What happened to your lovely wife?"

"Oh, she's been in a psychiatric hospital over 16 years," Ernesto answered.

"What about Demonesa's kids? Why can't they rearrange their lives for once and help you since they're the only beneficiaries of your inheritance?"

Ernesto shouted, furious, "They only came here to steal from me; they don't care about me—you and Gabriel are the only ones I trust." This is a good lesson to people who are rich and selfish and think they are better than others and will never be in need; they neglect people who truly love them in order to fit into society.

"Oh, really," said Evanjelica, "you only trust us to help you, but you didn't trust us when we needed you. When I was going through my divorce I didn't need your money; I just needed my father to stand up for me so I wouldn't have to fight against ex-husband alone. You turned your back on me. You gave Asmodeus more power over me to abuse me, wipe me clean of all my money and assets. You and your wife Demonesa went around telling the family I was stupid to allow my husband to steal from me, I was poor and would be knocking on peoples' doors asking for help. I was hurt when I heard this, and I decided to move myself away from family and not deal with anybody—to just focus on my children. I knew I had no money, that it was going to be hard, but I would not bother any family for help.

"I was blessed with dozens of good, true friends who stretched their helping hands to me and my boys. Even though they were not my blood I adopted them as my family. They've stood by my side and my kids when we were low down in the mud and they helped me stand on my feet, and they were there to see my children grow up and become successful and honorable young men. They were there for me when I opened my business, saw me grow and succeed, and they were there to celebrate my kids' and my own achievements. I did it all without the need of my rich family.

"I paid back the money my friends had loaned me in my time of need. I can never pay back their generosity and their loyalty. I can never pay them back their acts of kindness.

"Even though my friends are very wealthy, more so than you and your family, they never looked down on me or my kids; they saw us as human beings in need—that we were people, and that mattered to them more than our financial standing.

"Now, Father, I'll tell you this, get yourself to a priest and confess your sins, clear your conscience. You are over 80 years old and now it's time to reconcile with your past."

Ernesto was stubborn as he had always been just like Asmodeus. Both of them never admitted to being wrong; everyone else was wrong but them. He answered his daughter, "I don't have any sins and I never hurt anyone."

Ernesto never once apologized to his daughter. All he told her was that he never stood up for Asmodeus—that he was liar; Ernesto did not like that Asmodeus hit Evanjelica, and he was furious with Asmodeus for using Evanjelica as a bridge to a better life, and for leaving her empty-handed with two children to raise on her own. He also said he threw Asmodeus out of his house in Connecticut. One day Asmodeus went to visit Ernesto with a fake smile, and Ernesto heard Asmodeus was spreading bad rumors about Evanjelica and he was not happy with his son in-law.

Ernesto told Evanjelica, "Even though you and I were not speaking, you are still my daughter and I would never approve of Asmodeus's behavior. I was after him for a while to beat him up, not just for what he did to you. Asmodeus also spread lies between me and my family—nobody is talking to me." Evanjelica started to get emotional because for years she had thought her father supported Asmodeus's lies. Ernesto continued and said, "I loved your mother even after all these years and I can't stop thinking of her. I wish maybe one day I can see her again."

Evanjelica told her father, "You should have looked for her when she was alive; my mother is deceased now. She was not dead like you said she was many years ago. She is finally in paradise, a better place than you; she lived in hell her entire life in this sinful world." Evanjelica told her father that her mother forgave him and had asked Evanjelica to forgive her father before he died. She was a saint. "I'm nothing like her. I wish I was a better person; I just have a hard time forgiving a bad person who hurts the innocent.

"Because God is merciful, He forgives us, yes, but He wants us to repent, admit our faults, and ask Him for forgiveness. We need to admit our faults, ask for forgiveness, and be willing to amend our life, because if we do not ask to be forgiven, guess what? We go straight to hell."

Evanjelica knew she had sins; she was not perfect. One of her biggest sins was that it took her many years to forgive her father for what he did to her mother and brothers. And she did forgive her ex-husband Asmodeus for using her, as well as cheating on and stealing from her, but she had a hard time forgiving him for all the pain he'd caused in her boys' little hearts growing up and for not being there for them as a strong male figure, always with his ridiculous excuses. Evanjelica had sole custody of the boys and allowed Asmodeus to freely see the boys, but Orusula convinced him not to see them; she spent so much energy pursuing his ex-wife in court to dispute the child support payments.

Evanjelica reminded Orusula many times why she left Asmodeus because he was not a good husband to her or a good father to her children. *Why would she ever go back to him?* When Evanjelica discovered Asmodeus had a child with Orusula, Evanjelica even encouraged Asmodeus to support Orusula's child back in Portugal.

After the boys became adults and joined the military, Asmodeus wanted a relationship with his boys. Evanjelica encouraged the boys to show respect and have a relationship with him since he is their father. What she didn't know was that he just wanted to turn the boys' heads around, pit them against her, blaming her for everything like how she stopped him from visiting them. The boys knew their mother had them ready every Sunday, the only day Asmodeus asked for, and that he had failed to show up most times. The boys answered him, "How is that so? Mom had us ready and we all sat outside waiting for you for hours; you either didn't show or called with ridiculous excuses." After Evanjelica told all of this to her father Ernesto, she said, "So, you see, my father, how can I forgive a monster like Asmodeus? Unless I see he is sorry.

"I know I'm in sin—God wants us to forgive. And I forgave him for what he did to me, but I will only forgive him for the pain he caused my boys when I see he is truly sorry. He is not sorry. He keeps trying to turn people against me—my own sons I raised alone. He should be happy and grateful that my boys are good kids and should want a relationship with him, after all, he neglected them. I don't care about Asmodeus; he's nothing to me; let him think he's almighty without sin.

"I just want you, my father, to save your soul. it's time to be at peace with your conscience."

After hearing his daughter's kind words, Ernesto got emotional and told her, "You always had a good heart, Evanjelica, which helped you get through your difficult moments.

"I wish I had been there for you when you needed me. I lost a lot not seeing my grandsons grow up. I heard you did a good job raising them. Everyone who saw them told me your boys were very polite and treated people with respect. That made me proud and I'm proud of you, Evanjelica. You have always been smart, independent, and strong. I knew you would be okay raising your children alone."

Evanjelica got very emotional and cried; it was not really the apology she was looking for, yet she was happy to know and hear her father still had a heart worth saving and maybe with her prayers, eventually, Ernesto would come to his senses and admit his faults and save his soul.

Evanjelica told her father, "I cannot go back to Portugal. I'm struggling financially after the boys went into the military; they got married and I decided to relocate from the East Coast to the West Coast for a better climate. I wasn't lucky enough to find a good paying job. So I don't have that kind of money for a plane ticket. I will continue to pray for you, my father, and hope that one day we can all be together. Try to find peace in your heart, Dad," Evanjelica said as she hung up the phone. Evanjelica spent two hours talking with her father on an international call and ended up with an enormous phone bill. But she thought the call was worth it because a lot of things got cleared up that should have been cleared up a long time ago. Evanjelica felt more at peace with herself and it was big relief talking with her father knowing that a lot things Asmodeus had told her about her father were lies.

Chapter Twenty-two

Cross Country Adventure, 2018

After both her sons got married and were stationed far from home, Evanjelica knew her life would be different. The boys had their new families, and they would not be visiting her often, so there was no need to keep a big house for herself with all that work. After three years of dating Evanjelica, Paul talked about marriage often, yet he didn't want to move away from his siblings who all lived in Massachusetts. He still had his two adult children living at home, and he liked the cold winter, while Evanjelica liked warmer weather. Paul was a wonderful man who was proud of her and treated her with respect, and was always there when she needed him, but he didn't want move, nor was he fully ready for commitment, and Evanjelica didn't want to move to more freezing cold weather in Massachusetts. So, they went on with their lives in different directions and they stayed friends. Maybe sometime in the future they will have a mutual agreement in a place where they both would like to live. So, Evanjelica put her house on the market.

Evanjelica's friends also became closer to her knowing she was now alone, especially Angelina, her sister Jacinta, and her sons and godparents and their families who always included Evanjelica in all holiday events so she would not spend them alone. Jacinta was also divorced and as single working mother she understood Evanjelica better than anyone how hard it was to be a mother, father, and a provider. The two became close friends, more like sisters or better. Jacinta had a heart of gold; she would check on Evanjelica often, even though she was working so much, still having her two wonderful young children living at home. They lived 30 minutes from each other, but still Jacinta would invite Evanjelica over to her house, and asked her to bring her dog, so they could both can walk their dogs near their ocean. They also went to festivals together since neither had a husband.

Angelina was also a good soul with heart of gold to help everyone, but she was a married woman with children and grandchildren and a house always full of people. She was tireless, but occasionally she would get together with her sister Jacinta and Evanjelica. The three of them always had a great time when they got together. Evanjelica and Angelina worked in the electronics factory over 30 years ago when Evanjelica was still single and Angelina was married. Her son and daughter were toddlers back then and they later became godparents to Evanjelica's younger son Michael. They were friends and became even closer friends after Evanjelica came back from Portugal and rented an apartment from Angelina for a couple of years.

Angelina and her family stretched their helping hand to Evanjelica after her divorce and during all her surgeries, both when the boys were small and later after boys left. Evanjelica treasured their valuable friendship. No money in this entire world could ever repay Jacinta and Angelina for their generous gestures, acts of kindness, and support. Evanjelica had some amazing memories with them. Even though they were successful people and financially secure, they were not greedy, or selfish, or attracted to luxury and external success. Angelina and Jacinta were humble, genuine, and they were more attracted to internal values, kindness, and inner peace. That was priceless, and appealing to Evanjelica's eyes—she doesn't care for selfish greedy people.

Evanjelica built up a strong bond with many of her clients who loved her as a good friend and saw her boys grow up. Even after she closed her salon, sold the big equipment, and only kept the supplies, while relocating to West Coast, they remained supportive friends. But Jacinta and Angelina adopted Evanjelica as family.

She shipped her things to California where they stayed in storage in LA. After closing on the house, Evanjelica wanted to start her trip, but Angelina wanted Evanjelica to stay a few extra days and spend the Fourth of July with them. So, Jacinta invited Evanjelica to stay at her house till after the Fourth. Both Jacinta and Angelina wanted to spend as much time with her since this was such a long trip for Evanjelica and they would not see her for a while. It was soon time to say goodbyes. It's never easy to be apart from people we care about and love.

Evanjelica started her new adventure at 5 a.m. on July 5 since she wanted to beat the heat and traffic, leaving Connecticut taking route I-80/90 west.

She would stop every three to four hours of driving to stretch and shake her legs to prevent clots since she had a hip replacement two years prior to this trip.

After 10 hours of driving, she would stop and explore before getting up early to drive again. Evanjelica would send messages to Rafael in California, and Michael in Germany, as well as to all her friends in Connecticut who had faith in her, but were concerned about her traveling alone. She kept everyone updated of her travels that she was okay and the driving was going well.

Michael and Claudius, while stationed in Germany, traveled a lot around Europe before the birth of their daughter. Rafael had faith in his mother for taking this trip alone because he knew she was a tough woman. He and his wife Emily drove cross country as well in January 2014 after he'd completed his training in Pensacola. One thing Evanjelica always told her boys when they were younger was to travel as much as they could while single before starting a family, because after that it would get harder. When she was single she did lot a traveling around Europe then paused a while raising her children as a single struggling parent, thinking she'd lost hope of ever traveling again. So, she was happy she could do this trip.

Evanjelica spent the first night in Youngstown, Ohio, and then she continued the next morning to stop, stretch, and fill her gas tank in Chicago, spending the second night in Joliet, Illinois. She bought souvenirs at every stop, passing Iowa into 680 North

Omaha, and spent her third night in Denver and her fourth night in Green River, Utah; her last night was in spent in Tuscany Vegas, Nevada. She finally drove her last 300 miles from Las Vegas starting at 5 a.m., and arrived in Los Angeles by 11 a.m., where it took her two more hours to reach her destination, Thousand Oaks. She'd driven a full 3000 miles cross country, alone.

It was an amazing experience. Evanjelica made many trips via plane to California, Florida, and internationally to France, Span, and Portugal. Flying is beautiful being up in the sky above the clouds, but with driving you can see, feel, and smell the beauty nature has to offer. She must imagine it must be even more so if you're on a motorcycle.

Her road trip from France to Portugal in 1988, driving to Canada in between, and the cross country road trip East Coast to West Coast in 2018, exactly 30 years later, were both amazing experiences she treasures very much. The only thing she missed was not being able to take pictures of everything while she drove. Those scenes are stored in her memory.

Now 3000 miles distant from her ex-husband Asmodeus and Orusula who looked for every opportunity to humiliate and harass her, Evanjelica felt a new sense of freedom. She cried many tears for people who did not value or didn't appreciate her. Better alone than miserable. Being alone did not mean no one was interested in her, like Orusula's rumors; it simply meant Evanjelica was strong enough to encounter any challenge and overcome obstacles on her own.

Here was a lesson Evanjelica learned from her grandaunt, that she carried her entire life, passing it on to her children and all those she cared about. The saying went:

If you have a basket with ten apples and one apple is rotten, and you don't separate the nine good apples from the bad one, then the entire basket will go rotten and ten apples will go to waste. Just like with human beings. In a group of ten people there will be one evil-minded person who will try to poison the rest of the group; the other nine will have to choose whether they should stay bad, bully the other innocent people to impress this low-life miserable person, or they should be brave and separate themselves to be a better, stronger person. The bad apple, after doing some bad things, will find a way to quickly disappear and not get caught, while the remaining nine will get caught and take the blame.

Evanjelica knew when to separate herself from fake friends and negative surroundings. She chose never to participate in their nonsense. Yes, she was tormented terribly by these so-called "friends," but she knew that bullies are cowards and only strong when they are in a group that protects them.

***

Evanjelica was happy to finally reach her son's house. She stayed with them for a couple months as Rafael and Emily had asked her if they could all live together. Evanjelica did not think it was a good idea since a young couple needed to be on their own, and she also knew that the new generation won't follow or accept any parental advice unlike back in the day; it's best for everybody to be in their own place in order to continue having a good relationship. She would drop everything to help her children, and despite the fact that she wasn't wealthy, she would do what she could to stay in her own place. Children need to grow and mature on their own to learn to be responsible and independent like she had always been, and she would be there if they needed her—just under a different roof. After a couple of months she found a place and moved out to a different city, but was still close to her son.

Evanjelica liked California, but the jobs did not pay well enough to offset the cost of living. After a year there, Evanjelica relocated to Nevada in 2019, not her favorite state; she likes California better, and there's lot more green land in the Golden State, since Vegas is mostly desert. Her two friends Angelina and Jacinta came out to visit her, and like always they had a great time together. Most of Evanjelica's friends called or texted occasionally, but Jacinta and her sister Angelina called her daily knowing she was alone, wanting to be sure she was okay.

Evanjelica was only five hours' driving distance from her son, and was living now in a much bigger, brighter, and cheaper house, so she had to make the best of it. She had to register her car, change her driver's license, and update her cosmetology license again so she could work.

All of this was costing her money, as she was keeping her cosmetology license from all three states up to date not to let it expire. She learned a valuable lesson when she relocated to Portugal back when Asmodeus told her he did not like America. She didn't think she would come back and let her license expire. When she came back she could not work, and also had to pay the fines and spend additional hours in school. Never again would she let it expire.

She needed to find a job soon. She could always find a job as a hairstylist, but still needed a second income, which she did find as a QC inspector through a temporary job agency for a couple months. She was on and off of work, which made it hard with her health and physical issues. She didn't have a steady income, so she faced hardship, having no one to help her, and she was far away from everybody. Sometimes we put ourselves in situations not knowing how it will affect our own lives.

Chapter Twenty-three

A Novel is Born, 2020

It's not what she went through in life that defines who Evanjelica is—it's how she got through it that made her the person she is today. With all her health issues, injuries, and lack of income, Evanjelica faced hardship in Nevada. Only working part time in the salon was not enough to keep up with the expenses, even though rent was half of what it was in California, but car insurance in Vegas is high because it's a tourist city. She had to change her car registration, driver's license, and cosmetologist license again like she did in California so she could work. Things were going okay until the COVID-19 crisis closed all salons and everything else, and then she was completely out of work with no income and no family or friends around her. She was so isolated, and for an energetic person like Evanjelica, isolation was not good and it made her very depressed.

She would drive around the city to freshen her mind. There wasn't much traffic on the roads, which was so unusual for Vegas. All the casinos' parking lots were empty and the gates locked. It was sad and heartbreaking and it felt like the world had come to end. She'd head home even more depressed. A lot of things went through her mind—her past came flashing back to her—so she decided to grab her diary, all her notes, and just start writing to keep her mind busy. Evanjelica and Jacinta texted and talked on the phone daily with Evanjelica, and she kept complaining to Jacinta how bothered she was by the pandemic. Jacinta felt bad for her being all alone, far away from everybody and so isolated. When Evanjelica told Jacinta she decided writing a book would keep her mind busy, Jacinta immediately agreed with her and said, "Yes, there you go—you can do it! That's the best way to survive this isolation." And those were the words Evanjelica liked to hear, words of encouragement, unlike her relatives and false friends who kept telling her, "You cannot do it; you're not good at it." Well, she did it not to prove anybody wrong, but to prove to herself of her own capabilities. She's glad she has positive friends who believe in her and support her ideas.

Many times in her life, people told Evanjelica she couldn't do it, or that she wouldn't be good at something, yet she succeeded to become an American citizen, an inspector, and a cosmetologist. Then she thought maybe she should write a book. She was told before by many different people she couldn't that she needed to major in English, but she had so much free time on her hands now, she would try it. Testing her capacity to write her story, she found herself soon writing chapter after chapter. Throughout the writing process, she found inner peace so she could once again be in control of her life and her thoughts. Above all, she hopes this book inspires people to be determined and follow their dreams.

Evanjelica thought about the same lessons she gave her boys: do good, grow strong, and walk tall; do not waste time complaining about things or comparing your life to others and criticizing people. She also told them many times to change the 3 C's: Complaining, Criticizing Comparing, into 3 D's: Dedication, Devotion, and Determination. She was using them on herself now, letting go of Orusula, her major antagonist. Evanjelica continues to also pray for her father and Asmodeus, and all who have hurt her to someday come to their senses and soften their hearts, amend their lives, and save their souls.

Despite all her life struggles and suffering, Evanjelica feels blessed; she always meets kind people everywhere she goes. God replaced all things and the people she lost with better people, and kindness never goes out of style. She is eternally grateful for meeting so many kind people who stretched their helping hand to her in her time of need. We can repay favors, money, and material things, but most of all we can repay kindness with kindness and sacrifice for others as they sacrifice for us. We need to pray and thank the Lord for our blessings and for the kind people who cross our path in life.

Writing this book helped Evanjelica work the anger she'd held for many years out of her, helped her heal all the pain in her heart, and more importantly, helped her realize a lot of mistakes she'd made and lessons she'd learned: that everybody comes into our life for a reason or season. There are lessons we learn from bad people on what not to do, and we also learn from good people about how to be a better person and make better choices in our life.

She doesn't need the world to live; she only needs the One— Only the One who has power and control over the world. Every human being, every animal, and all living things on Planet Earth hold value, and are worthy of love and respect. No one deserves to be abused. We are all God's creation and we all have value.

The One has blessed Evanjelica in many different ways. Despite the fact she could not have children she became a mother of two miracles and wonderful sons and now has a beautiful granddaughter. She has faced financial hardship, depression, and has suffered physically and emotionally, and God always blesses her with strength to overcome all of life's obstacles. Friends of many years love her and she has met many people from prayer groups in church, jobs, and from all over the East and West Coasts who adore her and are happy to be around her.

Evanjelica cried a lot for many years, but her tears were not in vain. Her father Ernesto, who has been a cold and stubborn-hearted man, is slowly softening his heart through Evanjelica's prayers and forgiveness. He is accepting, not all, but some of his faults. Evanjelica has faith that someday Asmodeus and Orusula and all their enemies will also soften their hearts. She knows now that sin is the result of ignorance, weakness, and indifference. You can fool people on earth with lies, but you cannot fool God and she won't let discouragement and depression bring her down.

Evanjelica was bullied a great deal during her childhood and in her adult life—the harassment just never stopped. Being biracial, she was harassed in multiple ways by white people because she is partially Black and also by Black people because of her lighter skin. Evanjelica is not embarrassed by her skin pigmentation, or nationality, regardless of how many times she has been discriminated against; she is proud of who she is and proud of her background.

Racism and harassment are viruses—a severe disease that has lived in the veins of men and women for far too long. It's time for our moral immune system to get rid of it. There is no such thing as an evil person, but the belief that you are better than someone else because of the pigment of your skin is an evil idea. We should not be color blind; we should be color aware. Aware and willing to step up whenever or wherever we see racism.

Evanjelica's life is taking a different and positive turn that first started when she forgave her enemies and asked them for forgiveness, which helped her gain spiritual strength. Always forgive and never be afraid to ask for forgiveness. Always ask for blessings upon you and your loved ones. It's never too late to do the right thing and amend your life to do kindness.

Now Evanjelica needs to enjoy her life a little. Both of her sons always tell her, "It's your time now, Mom, take care of yourself, and enjoy life!" And she is—she is happy. She is blessed. She prays for herself, all her loved ones, and her enemies; may the Lord flood our souls, help us find the serenity we lost with difficulties that come, help us to calm down, clarify all situations of doubt and dispel our fears. May we all be blessed with positive energies, knowledge, wisdom, so our minds may be enlightened with clarity and truth, and in our hearts we will kindle the fire of Divine Love.

THE 3000 MILES HOME FOR THE HOLIDAYS

Santa came early to deliver Evanjelica her Christmas gift when she thought she was going to spend the 2020 holidays alone. Her son Rafael invited her on a cross country road trip from the West Coast to the East Coast. So she drove her own car behind her son, his wife Emily, and their dog, leaving California on a warm sunny day taking Route I-40 East into 81 North, into 87 E, driving through Nevada and Arizona. The hot temperatures turned to snow in New Mexico, followed by the rainy and windy miles in Texas, Oklahoma, Arkansas, and Tennessee. Virginia, Maryland, Pennsylvania, and New Jersey were cloudy but dry; they finally arrived safely in rainy Connecticut five days later.

In Connecticut Evanjelica spent some time with her best friend Jacinta, who missed her and was happy to see her back home, and she later met with her younger son, Michael, his daughter Cristina, and his wife, Claudius.

For first time in five years Evanjelica was in the same state with both her sons Rafael and Michael, and her granddaughter Cristina, for the holidays. Finally, this year they were all together. The two brothers, Rafael and Michael, due to their military careers, had been apart, one out of the country, and the other in a different state.

PRAYERS ANSWERED

Note: It is never too late to believe in prayers; it is never too late to turn to God for He truly loves us and He's the One in control of our life and destiny.

Evanjelica wishes everyone a healthy and prosperous New Year in 2021.

Hope you enjoyed this book and hope that you may benefit from it. Thank you for reading. Much love to you and yours. Blessings to all.

Acknowledgements

Special thanks from the author to all who helped me put this book together. All my friends from Connecticut are the most loyal and supportive friends who absolutely believed I would finish this book. Special thanks to my editor, Alice Osborn, who encouraged and guided me throughout the writing process. And thank you to Richard Dellamorte for his sharp eye and talented copyediting skills that added extra polish to my book.

I would like to thank David Parrish, of David Parrish Design, from Jacksonville, Florida, for his talents in designing my book's cover. Thank you to Michelle Argyle with Melissa Williams Design who did an incredible job with this book's interior design. Thank you to my good friends from Boulder City, Nevada who encouraged me to publish with Kindle Direct Publishing. Thank you to all the wonderful and patient Amazon staff members who made this book a reality.

Most of all, I'd like to thank my two sons, granddaughter, my dear siblings, and my family to whom I'm dedicating this novel.

About the Author

MARIA RIO had a dream to become a successful author, and to be an inspiration and make a difference in people's lives. A professionally trained and licensed cosmetologist and esthetician who owned a day spa for 18 years, she has also worked as a quality control inspector. All of this varied experience now feeds Maria's work as an author and storyteller who is now starting her second book. She is a family-oriented woman, having raised two wonderful sons on her own; she loves animals and her house is full of healthy plants and rocks of all different shapes, colors, and sizes. The author will never let a bird or homeless animal go hungry. Currently living in Las Vegas, Nevada, Maria thinks being a grandmother is the best thing in the world.

www.ingramcontent.com/pod-product-compliance
Lightning Source LLC
Chambersburg PA
CBHW060353110426
42743CB00036B/2904